OPPOSING VIEWPOINTS®

Paranormal Phenomena

Other Books of Related Interest

OPPOSING VIEWPOINTS®

Paranormal Phenomena

Mary E. Williams, *Book Editor*

Daniel Leone, *President*
Bonnie Szumski, *Publisher*
Scott Barbour, *Managing Editor*

OPPOSING
VIEWPOINTS®
SERIES

GREENHAVEN
PRESS®

THOMSON
✴
GALE

San Diego • Detroit • New York • San Francisco • Cleveland
New Haven, Conn. • Waterville, Maine • London • Munich

THOMSON

GALE

LIBRARY OF CONGRESS CATALOGING-IN-PUBLICATION DATA

Paranormal phenomena : opposing viewpoints / Mary E. Williams, book editor.
    p. cm. — (Opposing viewpoints series)
Includes bibliographical references and index.
ISBN 0-7377-1238-4 (lib. alk. paper) — ISBN 0-7377-1237-6 (pbk. : alk. paper)
    1. Parapsychology. I. Williams, Mary E., 1960– II. Opposing viewpoints series
(Unnumbered)
BF1031 .P334 2003
133—dc21   2002066461

Printed in the United States of America

"Congress shall make
no law. . . abridging the
freedom of speech, or of
the press."

First Amendment to the U.S. Constitution

The basic foundation of our democracy is the First
Amendment guarantee of freedom of expression.
The Opposing Viewpoints Series is dedicated to the
concept of this basic freedom and the idea that it is
more important to practice it than to enshrine it.

Contents

Why Consider Opposing Viewpoints?

*"The only way in which a human being can make some
approach to knowing the whole of a subject is by hearing
what can be said about it by persons of every variety of
opinion and studying all modes in which it can be looked
at by every character of mind. No wise man ever
acquired his wisdom in any mode but this."*

John Stuart Mill

In our media-intensive culture it is not difficult to find differing opinions. Thousands of newspapers and magazines
and dozens of radio and television talk shows resound with
differing points of view. The difficulty lies in deciding which
opinion to agree with and which "experts" seem the most
credible. The more inundated we become with differing
opinions and claims, the more essential it is to hone critical
reading and thinking skills to evaluate these ideas. Opposing
Viewpoints books address this problem directly by presenting stimulating debates that can be used to enhance and
teach these skills. The varied opinions contained in each
book examine many different aspects of a single issue. While
examining these conveniently edited opposing views, readers
can develop critical thinking skills such as the ability to
compare and contrast authors' credibility, facts, argumenta-
tion styles, use of persuasive techniques, and other stylistic
tools. In short, the Opposing Viewpoints Series is an ideal
way to attain the higher-level thinking and reading skills so
essential in a culture of diverse and contradictory opinions.

In addition to providing a tool for critical thinking, Opposing Viewpoints books challenge readers to question their
own strongly held opinions and assumptions. Most people
form their opinions on the basis of upbringing, peer pressure, and personal, cultural, or professional bias. By reading
carefully balanced opposing views, readers must directly
confront new ideas as well as the opinions of those with
whom they disagree. This is not to simplistically argue that

everyone who reads opposing views will—or should—change his or her opinion. Instead, the series enhances readers' understanding of their own views by encouraging confrontation with opposing ideas. Careful examination of others' views can lead to the readers' understanding of the logical inconsistencies in their own opinions, perspective on why they hold an opinion, and the consideration of the possibility that their opinion requires further evaluation.

Evaluating Other Opinions

To ensure that this type of examination occurs, Opposing Viewpoints books present all types of opinions. Prominent spokespeople on different sides of each issue as well as well-known professionals from many disciplines challenge the reader. An additional goal of the series is to provide a forum for other, less known, or even unpopular viewpoints. The opinion of an ordinary person who has had to make the decision to cut off life support from a terminally ill relative, for example, may be just as valuable and provide just as much insight as a medical ethicist's professional opinion. The editors have two additional purposes in including these less known views. One, the editors encourage readers to respect others' opinions—even when not enhanced by professional credibility. It is only by reading or listening to and objectively evaluating others' ideas that one can determine whether they are worthy of consideration. Two, the inclusion of such viewpoints encourages the important critical thinking skill of objectively evaluating an author's credentials and bias. This evaluation will illuminate an author's reasons for taking a particular stance on an issue and will aid in readers' evaluation of the author's ideas.

It is our hope that these books will give readers a deeper understanding of the issues debated and an appreciation of the complexity of even seemingly simple issues when good and honest people disagree. This awareness is particularly important in a democratic society such as ours in which people enter into public debate to determine the common good. Those with whom one disagrees should not be regarded as enemies but rather as people whose views deserve careful examination and may shed light on one's own.

Thomas Jefferson once said that "difference of opinion leads to inquiry, and inquiry to truth." Jefferson, a broadly educated man, argued that "if a nation expects to be ignorant and free . . . it expects what never was and never will be." As individuals and as a nation, it is imperative that we consider the opinions of others and examine them with skill and discernment. The Opposing Viewpoints Series is intended to help readers achieve this goal.

David L. Bender and Bruno Leone,
Founders

Greenhaven Press anthologies primarily consist of previously published material taken from a variety of sources, including periodicals, books, scholarly journals, newspapers, government documents, and position papers from private and public organizations. These original sources are often edited for length and to ensure their accessibility for a young adult audience. The anthology editors also change the original titles of these works in order to clearly present the main thesis of each viewpoint and to explicitly indicate the opinion presented in the viewpoint. These alterations are made in consideration of both the reading and comprehension levels of a young adult audience. Every effort is made to ensure that Greenhaven Press accurately reflects the original intent of the authors included in this anthology.

Introduction

"After working with 20 or so [alien] abductees, . . . it became clear to me that I was dealing with a phenomenon that could not be explained psychiatrically."
—*John E. Mack*

"The best explanation for many abduction experiences is that they are elaborations of the experience of sleep paralysis."
—*Susan Blackmore*

Kate, a woman profiled by journalist Marcia Jedd in a 1997 *Fate* magazine article, claims to have pleasant memories of small, gray humanoids visiting her throughout her childhood. These beings often peered into her family's Michigan farmhouse at night, and on occasion visited and talked with her in her room, Kate maintains. She professes, however, that she became afraid of the beings as she grew up and realized that other children were not having similar experiences. When a minister she consulted at age fifteen reacted negatively to her stories about contact with the gray creatures, she buried her memories and refused to talk about the visitations for twenty-eight years. Yet Kate asserts that she continued to encounter the beings, who would periodically appear, take her on board an alien spacecraft, and conduct medical examinations. Eventually Kate began exploring specific incidents of contact with the beings while under hypnosis. Now in her fifties, she believes that the aliens have always been with her. "The beings told me they did things to me before I was born. I believe my abductions happened as a result of pre-birth contact," she states.

While Kate's story is astonishing, it is not unique. An estimated nineteen million Americans say that they have seen a UFO. Moreover, a controversial 1991 Roper poll claims that up to four million people have experienced the alien abduction phenomenon.

Researchers' reactions to reports from people claiming to have been abducted and subjected to experiments by aliens il-

lustrate the debate between parapsychologists an&
Skeptical scientists reject the existence of such ph
on the grounds that there is no convincing scientifi
They decry belief in the paranormal as an example of
scientific attitude that promotes disdain for the principles of
logic and reason. However, parapsychologists and others who
explore unexplained phenomena contend that there is overwhelming anecdotal evidence to suggest that many of these
phenomena are real. They maintain that rejecting the possibility of the existence of the paranormal is itself unscientific.

John E. Mack, a Harvard University psychiatrist who has
studied and published books on the abduction phenomenon,
contends that physical evidence and similarities between abductees' stories supports the validity of abductee accounts.
In a typical case, the abductee awakens in a state of paralysis
with a feeling that there is an alien presence in the room.
Unable to resist, he or she is levitated from the bedroom and
taken to an awaiting spaceship. The experiencer is subjected
to an examination in which samples of hair, skin, sperm or
ova, and other tissues are taken and a tracking device is implanted. Finally, the abductee is returned to his or her room
with all conscious memories of the experience erased (only
later to be recovered with the help of hypnosis). Mack notes
that most abductees are ordinary, healthy people who have
no apparent reason for deception and who are not seeking
the public limelight. He maintains that the abductees he has
studied were "quite sane [and] had come forth reluctantly,
fearing the discrediting of their stories or outright ridicule."

To further support his claim that the alien abduction phenomenon is genuine, Mack points to physical evidence such
as signs of psychological trauma among experiencers, physical scars, and "implants" (foreign objects removed from abductees' bodies). He contends that the trauma exhibited by
abductees is not the result of psychosis or fantasy and therefore must have a basis in real experience. As for the implants,
he argues that electrochemical tests have failed to identify
them as being of earthly origin, leaving open the possibility
that they are extraterrestrial. "In virtually every case," Mack
asserts, "there are one or more concrete physical findings
that accompany or follow the abduction experience."

Supporters of the abduction theory have various hypotheses about the aliens' purpose in kidnapping humans. Some, like Mack, believe that aliens have arrived as part of an ultimately benevolent plan to bring about a spiritual awakening and a profound change in human consciousness. Others think that aliens are conducting a vast breeding program to create a hybrid alien-human species—*homo alienus*—that will eventually populate and take over the earth.

Skeptics argue, however, that there is no conclusive evidence to support the alien abduction and breeding theory. Most contend that it is extremely unlikely that intelligent beings capable of interstellar travel exist on other planets. Therefore, they maintain, consideration of otherworldly kidnappers as the explanation for the abductee phenomenon is beyond the pale of science and reason.

Acclaimed skeptic Susan Blackmore, a psychology lecturer at the University of the West of England, argues that there are simpler and more plausible explanations for the experiences of alleged abductees. For one thing, she points out, the often-cited Roper poll claim that four million people believe they have been abducted by aliens is based on a seriously misleading interpretation of data. The poll never asked respondents to answer the question "have you ever been abducted by aliens?" Instead, respondents were asked if they had had certain "indicator experiences," such as "waking up paralyzed with a sense of a strange presence in the room," feelings of flying through the air, experiencing periods of lost time, and discovering puzzling scars but not remembering how the scars were received. Respondents who answered "yes" to a certain number of indicator experiences were said to be alien abductees. Blackmore maintains that the poll is severely flawed because it assumes that certain common experiences might be signs of alien abduction.

Interestingly, one of the Roper poll's so-called indicators—waking up paralyzed—does offer a clue about the real source of the alien abduction phenomenon, asserts Blackmore. A relatively common sleep disorder known as sleep paralysis is probably what alleged abductees are suffering from, she contends. Normal sleep brings on a harmless paralysis of muscles that prevents people from acting out on their dreams. But about one in five people has experiences of waking from sleep while this paralysis persists. Such sleep paralysis, Blackmore maintains, is often accompanied by hallucinations or by a related sleep disturbance called false awakening, in which people dream that they have awakened but in fact are still dreaming. With prevailing cultural myths about UFOs and extraterrestrials, she contends, it is no wonder that people today dream about being abducted by aliens. Many past cultures also concocted myths to explain sleep paralysis, such as the tale of the incubus and succubus—"demons" who sexually violated their sleeping victims.

Blackmore discounts Mack's claim that alien-designed "implants" provide proof of abduction, as no evidence has arisen proving that the objects are extraterrestrial. In fact, skeptics point out, a few pathology labs that have analyzed such objects have concluded that they were compacted pieces of human tissue. Moreover, alleged abductees' "unexplained" physical scars could have entirely mundane causes—active and busy people often forget the origin of a scar, Blackmore and others contend. In the absence of extraordinary evidence to support claims of extraterrestrial kidnappings, Blackmore and other skeptical researchers maintain that hallucinations related to sleep disorders should be accepted as the most likely explanation of the abductee phenomenon.

"Extraordinary claims require extraordinary evidence," skeptics often say. Without solid scientific proof of the existence of the paranormal, they argue, phenomena such as UFOs or alien abductions should be considered hallucinations or fantasies. Devotees of the paranormal, however, often maintain that the skeptics' outright rejection of the possibility of the existence of paranormal phenomena is in itself unscientific. In the chapters: Is Belief in Paranormal Phenomena Unscientific? Is There Proof That Paranormal Phenomena Exist? Are UFOs Extraterrestrial Spacecraft? Does Life After Death Exist? *Paranormal Phenomena: Opposing Viewpoints* explores the fascinating debate between doubters of and believers in the supernatural.

CHAPTER 1

Is Belief in Paranormal Phenomena Unscientific?

Chapter Preface

The commercial success of television and cable shows dramatizing investigations of the paranormal, such as *The X-Files* and *Psi Factor*, has led to the creation of other broadcast features focusing on UFOs, government conspiracies, haunted houses, psychics, and angels. Documentaries about paranormal phenomena appear regularly on cable channels that feature educational and historical programs. At the same time, belief in the existence of paranormal phenomena has become widespread. According to surveys by Gallup, CNN, and *USA Today*, 70 percent of Americans believe in miracles and angels, 50 percent believe in ESP, and between 20 and 50 percent believe in astrology, ghosts, and communication with the dead. Skeptics, media researchers, and enthusiasts of the paranormal dispute whether the entertainment industry contributes to Americans' belief in the supernatural.

The Committee for Scientific Investigation of Claims of the Paranormal (CSICOP) decries the influence of television in promoting what they call unscientific beliefs. "A lot of people believe [in the paranormal] because it's on television," maintains Paul Kurtz, chairman of CSICOP. According to a 1997 survey conducted by media researcher Glenn Sparks, people who regularly watch shows like *Sightings* "were significantly more likely than [nonwatchers] to endorse paranormal beliefs." Many scientists and skeptics are especially concerned that documentary-style shows that emphasize belief in the supernatural contribute to a dangerous level of scientific illiteracy among Americans.

Sparks points out, however, that some research indicates that documentaries presenting the opinions of both skeptics and nonskeptics actually result in a decrease in paranormal beliefs. In addition, shows that include disclaimers such as "the following story is based on reported incidents" or "these depicted events violate the known laws of nature" lead viewers to doubt the existence of the paranormal. "Certain types of messages may promote paranormal beliefs," Sparks maintains. "But the flip-side is that other types of messages may help to promote critical thinking and to discourage easy acceptance of ridiculous ideas."

Fans of the paranormal argue that rather than fostering superstition, documentaries and dramas about the supernatural merely provide entertainment. Chris Carter, creator and producer of *The X-Files*, maintains that the stories for his show are drawn from already existing beliefs in the paranormal. But, he asserts, "It's fiction . . . we make this stuff up." Others contend that speculation about the paranormal helps to fulfill a widespread need for mystery in an increasingly rational and mechanistic world.

While some scientists express concern that the portrayal of paranormal phenomena on television contributes to an antiscientific attitude among viewers, those who produce and watch such programs argue that the shows simply draw on imaginative material from popular culture. The authors in the following chapter debate whether belief in the existence of paranormal phenomena is unscientific.

| *"Specific harms caused by paranormal beliefs [include] a decline in scientific literacy and critical thinking."*

Belief in Paranormal Phenomena Is Unscientific

Melissa Pollak

In the following viewpoint, Melissa Pollak argues that the widespread belief in paranormal phenomena such as ESP, ghosts, and UFOs reveals a decline in critical thinking skills among Americans. The scientific illiteracy exhibited in paranormal beliefs is detrimental to a culture that relies on an informed public to solve society's problems, Pollak maintains. Some scientists insist that the entertainment industry's promotion of paranormal topics is partly responsible for the increase in pseudoscientific beliefs. The media should therefore be encouraged to advance the understanding of science and scientific concepts. Pollak is a researcher with the National Science Foundation's Division of Science Resource Studies.

As you read, consider the following questions:
1. In Pollak's opinion, what is the difference between science literacy and scientific literacy?
2. What percentage of Americans believe in ESP, according to surveys cited by the author?
3. According to Pollak, what two awards were established to promote scientific responsibility in the media?

D oes it matter if people believe in astrology, extrasensory perception (ESP), or that aliens have landed on Earth? Are people who check their horoscopes, call psychic hotlines, or follow stories about alien abductions just engaging in harmless forms of entertainment? Or are they displaying signs of scientific illiteracy?

Concerns have been raised, especially in the science community, about widespread belief in paranormal phenomena. Scientists (and others) have observed that people who believe in the existence of paranormal phenomena may have trouble distinguishing fantasy from reality. Their beliefs may indicate an absence of critical thinking skills necessary not only for informed decisionmaking in the voting booth and in other civic venues (for example, jury duty), but also for making wise choices needed for day-to-day living.

The Harms of Pseudoscience

Specific harms caused by paranormal beliefs have been summarized as:

- a decline in scientific literacy and critical thinking;
- the inability of citizens to make well-informed decisions;
- monetary losses (psychic hotlines, for example, offer little value for the money spent);
- a diversion of resources that might have been spent on more productive and worthwhile activities (for example, solving society's serious problems);
- the encouragement of a something-for-nothing mentality and that there are easy answers to serious problems, for example, that positive thinking can replace hard work; and
- false hopes and unrealistic expectations.

For a better understanding of the harms associated with pseudoscience, it is useful to draw a distinction between science literacy and scientific literacy. The former refers to the possession of technical knowledge. Scientific literacy, on the other hand, involves not simply knowing the facts, but also requires the ability to think logically, draw conclusions, and make decisions based on careful scrutiny and analysis of those facts.

The amount of information now available can be overwhelming and seems to be increasing exponentially. This has led to "information pollution," which includes the presentation of fiction as fact. Thus, being able to distinguish fact from fiction has become just as important as knowing what is true and what is not. The lack of this ability is what worries scientists (and others), leading them to conclude that pseudoscientific beliefs can have a detrimental effect on the wellbeing of society.

How Common Is Belief in the Paranormal?

Belief in the paranormal seems to be widespread. Various polls have shown that

- As many as one-third of Americans believe in astrology, that is, that the position of the stars and planets can affect people's lives. In 1999, 7 percent of those queried in the National Science Foundation (NSF) survey said that astrology is "very scientific" and 29 percent answered "sort of scientific." Twelve percent said they read their horoscope every day or "quite often"; 32 percent answered "just occasionally."
- Nearly half or more believe in extrasensory perception or ESP. According to one poll, the number of people who have consulted a fortuneteller or a psychic may be increasing: in 1996, 17 percent of the respondents reported contact with a fortuneteller or psychic, up from 14 percent in 1990.
- Between one-third and one-half of Americans believe in unidentified flying objects (UFOs). A somewhat smaller percentage believes that aliens have landed on Earth.

Other polls have shown one-fifth to one-half of the respondents believing in haunted houses and ghosts, faith healing, communication with the dead, and lucky numbers. Some surveys repeated periodically even show increasing belief in these examples of pseudoscience.

Belief in most—but not all—paranormal phenomena is higher among women than men. More women than men believe in ESP (especially telepathy and precognition), astrology, hauntings, and psychic healing. On the other hand, men have stronger beliefs in UFOs and bizarre life forms, for example, the Loch Ness monster. In the NSF survey, 39 percent of the women, compared with 32 percent of the men, said astrology is "very" or "sort of" scientific; 56 percent of the women, compared with 63 percent of the men, answered "not at all scientific."

Not surprisingly, belief in astrology is negatively associated with level of education. Among those without high school diplomas, only 41 percent said that astrology is "not at all scientific." The comparable percentages for high school and college graduates are 60 percent and 76 percent, respectively.

The Role of the Media

Scientists and others believe that the media—and in particular, the entertainment industry—may be at least partially responsible for the large numbers of people who believe in astrology, ESP, alien abductions, and other forms of pseudoscience. Because not everyone who watches shows with paranormal themes perceives such fare as merely entertaining fiction, there is concern that the unchallenged manner in which some mainstream media portray paranormal activities is exacerbating the problem and contributing to the public's scientific illiteracy. In recent years, studies have been undertaken to determine whether televised depictions of paranormal events and beliefs influence television viewers' conceptions of reality. Although the results of these studies are tentative and require replication, all of them suggest that the way television presents paranormal subjects does have an effect on what viewers believe. For example,

- Those who regularly watch shows like *The X-Files, Unsolved Mysteries*, and *Sightings* were significantly more likely than those who did not watch these programs to endorse paranormal beliefs.
- Shows about paranormal phenomena, including UFOs, without disclaimers are more likely than those with disclaimers to foster belief in the paranormal.
- Some fans of *The X-Files* find the show's storylines "highly plausible," and also believe that the government is currently conducting clandestine investigations similar to those depicted on the series.

The Committee for the Scientific Investigation of Claims of the Paranormal (CSICOP) is a nonprofit scientific and educational organization started in 1976 by scientists (including several Nobel laureates), members of the academic community, and science writers. Members of CSICOP, frequently referred to as skeptics, advocate the scientific investigation of paranormal claims and the dissemination of factual information to counter those claims.

Piraro. © 1996 by Dan Piraro. Reprinted with permission.

CSICOP's mission includes taking advantage of opportunities to promote critical thinking, science education, and the use of reason to determine the merits of important issues.

Promoting Media Responsibility

The Council for Media Integrity, an educational outreach and advocacy program of CSICOP, was established in 1996. Its objective is to promote the accurate depiction of science by the media. The Council, which includes distinguished international scientists, academics, and members of the media, believes it is necessary to counteract the entertainment industry's portrayal of paranormal phenomena because:

- television has such a pervasive impact on what people believe;
- an increasing number of shows are devoted to the paranormal, and they attract large audiences;
- a number of shows use a documentary style to promote belief in the reality of UFOs, government coverups, and alien abductions;
- opposing views are seldom heard in shows that advocate belief in the paranormal; and
- some shows contribute to scientific illiteracy by promoting unproven ideas and beliefs as real, instilling a distrust of scientists and fostering misunderstanding of the methods of scientific inquiry.

To promote media responsibility—particularly within the entertainment industry—and to publicize irresponsibility—the Council established two awards:

- The "Candle in the Dark Award" is given to television programs that have made a major contribution to advancing the public's understanding of science and scientific principles. The 1997 and 1998 awards went to two PBS programs: *Bill Nye The Science Guy* and *Scientific American Frontiers.*
- The "Snuffed Candle Award" is given to television programs that impede public understanding of the methods of scientific inquiry. The 1997 and 1998 winners were Dan Akroyd, for promoting the paranormal on the show *Psi-Factor,* and Art Bell, whose radio talk-show promoted belief in UFOs and alien abductions.

In its efforts to debunk pseudoscience, the Council also urges TV producers to label documentary-type shows depicting the paranormal as either entertainment or fiction, provides the media with the names of expert spokespersons, asks U.S. newspapers to print disclaimers with horoscope columns, and uses "media watchdogs" to monitor programs and encourage responsibility on the part of television producers.

Finally, various skeptics groups and renowned skeptic James Randi have long-standing offers of large sums of money to anyone who can prove a paranormal claim. Randi and members of his "2000 Club" are offering more than a million dollars. So far, no one has met the challenge.

"[One] person who studies parapsychology [may be] pseudoscientific, but that does not mean that it is impossible for some other person to carry out a study in the same field that is truly scientific."

The Study of Paranormal Phenomena Can Be Scientific

Peter A. Sturrock

Peter A. Sturrock is a professor of space science and astrophysics at Stanford University and the director of the university's Center for Space Science and Astrophysics. In the following viewpoint, Sturrock contends that the examination of so-called paranormal phenomena need not be—as many scientists have claimed—unscientific. All topics, including those that challenge accepted ideas, can be investigated with scientific knowledge and techniques. He concludes that responsible scientists should maintain a curious and critical attitude and avoid labeling paranormal phenomena as unworthy of scientific inquiry.

As you read, consider the following questions:

1. What three modes of thought do scientists need, in Sturrock's opinion?
2. In the author's view, what is the problem with the term "paranormal"?
3. How did Galileo challenge the accepted knowledge of his day, according to Sturrock?

From "Curious, Creative, and Critical Thinking: The Responsible Approach to Exploring the Unknown," by Peter A. Sturrock, *Truth Seeker*, vol. 124. Copyright © 1997 by Society for Scientific Exploration. Reprinted with permission.

E dward Ginzion, one of the founders of Varian Associ- ates, once remarked, concerning his colleague Russell Varian, that "he had several modes of thought, of which log- ical thinking was only one." So it is, most likely, with all great inventors, and so it is, I believe, with all truly produc- tive scientists. In this essay, I will argue that scientists need at least three modes of thought that I call curious, creative, and critical.

These requirements, though they may be quite general in their applicability, come sharply in focus when one deals with anomalies within mainstream science or with anoma- lous phenomena that seem to reside outside of science as we know it.

What Is Scientific?

An even more disturbing and challenging situation arises if a scientist takes an interest in a topic that is outside of main- stream science, and is believed by the scientific community to represent "pseudoscience," the "paranormal," or "patho- logical science." Some of the best known examples that are regarded in this light are "parapsychology," "ufology" (the study of UFO reports) and "cryptozoology," the search for zoological anomalies (including the search for Big Foot and for the so-called "Loch Ness Monster"). Even the mention of such terms will send a shudder through the frame of al- most any self-respecting scientist. Why is this so?

Typical responses to this question are in fact indicated by the terms I have just used. If I assert that a subject is "pseu- doscience," I am stating that the activity is not truly scien- tific but merely pretends to be scientific. However, such an assertion is indefensible. A "subject" is neither scientific nor nonscientific. It is only the study carried out by a particular person or group of persons that can be so described. Hence one may be able to make a case that this person who studies parapsychology is being pseudoscientific, but that does not mean that it is impossible for some other person to carry out a study in the same field that is truly scientific and meets the highest standards of the scientific enterprise.

There is a similar problem connected with the term "paranormal." If I assert that a subject is "paranormal," I am implying that I know what is "normal." I am further implying that any subject that is not "normal," according to my definition of the term, does not accord with scientific knowledge, and must be rejected as bogus. This would be a huge responsibility to take on. Most scientists would agree that science is incomplete. They would agree with Isaac Newton who stated that he felt like a person who had found a few beautiful pebbles from the shore, while huge oceans lay unexplored before him. If we do not know all there is to know about the universe (including human beings and everything else in the universe), then clearly we cannot claim to know what is "normal," and it is therefore foolish to use the term "paranormal." Such issues are perceived as heretical precisely because they involve a combination of intellectual and political considerations.

Challenges to Understanding and Power

Indeed, my understanding of the term "heresy" is the following: *A heresy is a proposition that is, at the same time, a challenge to understanding and a challenge to power.* Galileo faced the investigators of the Holy Inquisition as a result of his assertion that the Ptolemaic model of the solar system, in which the Earth is at rest and all bodies revolve around the Earth, is wrong, and that the Copernican model, that places the Sun at the center and has the Earth revolve around the Sun, is correct. Perhaps more important was his assertion that we may discover truth about the universe by observation, rather than through the reading of Holy Scripture. In addition to the purely intellectual challenge of offering a new model of the solar system, Galileo was challenging the Church as the ultimate source and judge of truth. Galileo was thereby challenging the status and power of the Church.

One may discern a similar conflict in relation to fields such as parapsychology. The very term "parapsychology" is unfortunate, since it gives the impression that it is somehow related to "psychology." This therefore implies that psychologists should know whether or not there is anything to this subject. Since psychologists, in fact, know very little about parapsychology, this creates a situation of some tension.

One can imagine that the public and the news media

could implicitly or explicitly criticize the psychological community for not realizing early on that there was something to parapsychology, and the psychological community would, to some extent, lose face. Hence the conflict between parapsychological investigators and mainstream psychologists is not unlike the conflict between Galileo and the Church. Whether or not these investigators will prove to be correct in their assertions, as Galileo has been proved to be correct, remains to be seen, but the ultimate truth or falsity of a proposition is not, in my opinion, a relevant consideration in trying to determine whether or not a challenge is heresy.

Experts Can Be Wrong

We have all heard stories of how the experts have been wrong, time and again. We forget that the experts often merely parrot the conventional wisdom of the time and have no expertise beyond what the lay public possesses.

We in the UFO community often point to the fact that the French Academy of sciences, at the beginning of the nineteenth century, rejected the idea that rocks could fall from the sky. Everyone knows that there are no rocks in the sky, and those who suggest otherwise must be deluded, insane, lying, or simply mistaken.

What we rarely talk about is how the French Academy of sciences reversed itself in 1803 when a proper scientific study, along with physical evidence, was offered, proving that rocks [meteors] could fall from the sky. Jean-Baptiste Biot published his report, and the scientific community in France accepted his study.

Kevin D. Randle, *Scientific Ufology*, 1999.

Linda Pauling, daughter of the famous chemist Linus Pauling, once asked her father "How is it you had so many good ideas?" to which he replied, "I had many more ideas, and threw away all the bad ones."

As the astrophysicist Tommy Gold once remarked, "Old ideas are not right simply because they are old, and new ideas are not wrong simply because they are new."

Carl Sagan was correct in asserting that "extraordinary claims require extraordinary evidence," but that does not mean that anything less than extraordinary evidence may be ignored.

Off Limits

There is, at present, a huge no-man's-land between established science, on the one hand, and the public and news media, on the other hand. In this area one may find topics such as parapsychology, ufology and cryptozoology. The public is curious and wants answers to these questions. The average citizen does not have the technical skills necessary to resolve these mysteries. The scientific community, on the other hand, has a store of knowledge and an arsenal of techniques that could be brought to bear on these problems, but this is not happening because the scientific community views these subjects as being "off limits." Such topics are "beyond the pale."

The Society for Scientific Exploration was founded in 1982 to help redress this situation. The Society offers a forum, through its meetings and through its journal, the *Journal of Scientific Exploration*, for the presentation of results of serious investigations into any topic amenable to such study. There have, to date, been no major breakthroughs in the sense of research that establishes the reality and nature of any of these phenomena. On the other hand, our knowledge of these phenomena is slowly improving. Our insight is increasing. It is my conviction that if we persevere with the judicious application of curious, creative and critical thinking, it will be only a matter of time before each of these enigmas is finally resolved.

> *"The contemporary skeptical movement . . . provides a much-needed antidote to the persistence of irrational, paranormal, and occult systems of belief."*

Paranormal Phenomena Should Be Approached with Skepticism

Paul Kurtz

In the following viewpoint, Paul Kurtz maintains that reports about so-called paranormal events are best approached with an attitude of skeptical inquiry. Fantastic claims about the existence of psychic powers, faith healing, UFOs, and other unusual phenomena have thus far not been verified by solid scientific evidence, he points out. Those who believe in the paranormal tend to rely on anecdotes and testimony—which are unreliable—or may be influenced by fantasy and wishful thinking. In contrast, the skeptic recognizes that there is generally a natural explanation for anomalous events. Kurtz is a former philosophy professor and founder of the Committee for the Scientific Investigation of Claims of the Paranormal.

As you read, consider the following questions:
1. Why did Kurtz establish the Committee for the Scientific Investigation of Claims of the Paranormal?
2. Through her experiments, what did psychologist Elizabeth Loftus discover about the nature of memory, according to Kurtz?
3. In John Schumaker's view, why do humans have a hunger for transcendence?

The contemporary skeptical movement may be said to have been initiated with the founding of the Committee for the Scientific Investigation of Claims of the Paranormal [CSICOP] in 1976. This movement is now growing worldwide and it provides a much-needed antidote to the persistence of irrational, paranormal, and occult systems of belief. . . .

The Need for Skeptical Inquiry

Permit me to say something about the reasons why I decided to create such a movement. I had long been a critic of paranormal (and supernatural) claims that could not be supported by the evidence. I was astonished that many or most of the claims continued to enjoy widespread public support, even though they had been refuted. Moreover, the mass media latched onto paranormal claims, which they discovered was profitable at the box office. Uri Geller, Jeane Dixon, and others were enjoying a huge following with hardly a dissent. This occurred despite the fact that scientific inquiry, which investigated their claims, had rejected them for lack of evidence. Astrology is a good case in point, for it was refuted by astronomers, physicists, statisticians, psychologists, and other scientists. There is no empirical basis for horoscopes or sun-sign astrology; its cosmology is based on the discredited Ptolemaic system; moreover, it is possible to test its predictions and forecasts, and the results are invariably negative. Yet very few in the general public are aware of these criticisms, and indeed often confuse astronomy with astrology.

With this in mind, I helped to draft and issue a statement, "Objections to Astrology," with the assistance of Bart Bok, a noted astronomer, and Lawrence Jerome, a science writer. This statement was endorsed by 186 leading scientists, including nineteen Nobel Laureates. It received immediate worldwide attention, especially after the *New York Times* did a front-page story. It seemed to me that the success of this effort, especially within the scientific community, called for the need for a more organized response by the academic and scientific community. I decided to create a new coalition comprised of scientists, skeptics, philosophers, magicians, and others. Hence, I invited several dozen critics of the paranormal to Amherst, New York, to an open conference to develop an organized opposition to the uncontested growth of belief in the paranormal. . . .

The conference was held at the new campus of the State University of New York at Buffalo, in Amherst, New York. At that time, I was editor of *The Humanist* magazine, one of the leading journals critical of religion. At the inaugural meeting of CSICOP, in my opening address ("The Scientific Attitude versus Anti-Science and Pseudoscience"), I said that there was a long-standing conflict in the history of culture between religion and science, but that today a new challenge to science has come to the fore because of the growth of pseudoscientific and paranormal claims. The apparent popular belief in exorcism, nouveau witches, and Satanism were symptomatic of the Aquarian consciousness then being proclaimed. The mass media also presented as true (and usually without any dissent) accounts of Kirlian photography, the wonders of ESP and psychokinesis, UFO sightings, the Bermuda Triangle, Bigfoot, van Däniken's *Chariots of the Gods*, etc. A great number of quasi-religious organizations had emerged at that time, including Hare Krishna, Reverend Moon, and the Scientologists. These were symptomatic of a countercultural opposition to science that had begun to appear, and it needed, in my judgment, to be responded to—for the public had a right to hear the scientific critique of pseudoscientific and fringe claims.

I raised the following questions: *Should we assume that the scientific revolution, which began in the sixteenth century, is continuous? Or will it be overwhelmed by the forces of unreason?*

And I replied: *We ought not to assume, simply because ours is an advanced scientific-technological society, that irrational thinking will he overcome. The evidence suggests that this is far from being the case. Indeed, there is always the danger that science itself may be engulfed by the forces of unreason.*

Since that time, postmodernism has emerged, denying the possibility of scientific objectivity, and considering science as only one mythic narrative among others. And much to everyone's surprise there have been widespread attacks on the Enlightenment and the ideals of the scientific revolution.

Today these antiscientific protests are accompanied by a

resurgence of fundamentalist religions. So the challenge to science is not simply from propagandists for the paranormal, but also from the disciples of many religions. I should point out that although I personally believe that skeptics need to deal with religious claims as well as with paranormal claims, I recommended that CSICOP concentrate on paranormal and pseudoscientific claims. . . .

The Meaning of "Paranormal"

First, the term *paranormal* itself is highly questionable. We decided to use the term only because proponents (such as J.B. Rhine) had used it. We doubt that it is possible to find a paranormal realm separate from or independent of the natural universe. We are seeking normal and natural explanations for phenomena. The best meaning of the term *paranormal* is that there are some times bizarre, unexpected *anomalies* that we encounter (as Charles Fort described them), and we are willing to examine them with an open mind, and do not wish to reject them *a priori* and antecedent to inquiry. Murray Gell-Mann, Nobel Prize–winner and a Fellow of CSICOP, at a conference at the University of Colorado in 1986, observed that in one sense we deny the paranormal entirely, because once we find that phenomena can be explained by reference to prosaic causes, then these explanations are incorporated into the natural scientific world-view, and are not separated from it. I reiterate, we have an open mind and are willing to examine anomalies without prejudgment, providing that the claims made by the proponents are responsible.

Anecdotes and Testimony

Anecdotal reports: What we have found is that many reports of anomalous events are based on anecdotal accounts. While these reports cannot be dismissed out of hand or without a fair hearing, especially if they are seriously offered, skeptics hold that inquirers should go beyond mere anecdotes to a more systematic examination of the phenomena. Many anecdotal narratives are based upon private experiences, subjective and introspective in character, or upon memory of past events, which may be unreliable, or made upon second- or third-hand hearsay.

It is important that all such reports be carefully sifted through, if possible, before they are accepted. Anecdotes may have a grain of truth and they may bring new and important data, otherwise overlooked. On the other hand, they may involve serious misperception or faulty memory; they may involve stories embellished upon beyond their original meaning; or they may be incidents blown out of proportion to what actually happened, or the deception of the senses colored by suggestion. Many of these alleged anecdotes, if reported second-hand, take on the character of gossip, folk tales, or urban legends. There is a tendency for people who believe in the occult to read mysterious nuances into otherwise prosaic experiences, or to exaggerate the significance of random events. This commonly occurs, for example, in reports of ghostly apparitions, crisis premonitions of death, visitations by extraterrestrial beings, or the accuracy of psychic prophecies. Skeptics ask, Did the event occur as the person states, and Is the interpretation placed on the event the most likely cause?

Unless an anecdotal account can be corroborated independently, investigators urge caution about its authenticity. This not only applies to the truth of the event alleged to have actually occurred, but to the occult explanation that is imposed on it because of ignorance of the real causes.

The skeptic says that the report may or may not be true and that if it did occur there may be alternative causal explanations to be made of it. Are we dealing with a real event, or a misperception, hallucinatory experience, fantasy, and/or a misinterpretation of what happened?

Eyewitness testimony: The appeal to eyewitness testimony is the bedrock of our knowledge about the world and ourselves. The data is drawn from direct first-hand experience. It is important, however, that such testimony not be accepted on face value without careful inspection. This is especially the case when the testimony is about anomalous, unexpected, or bizarre events. If a person reports that it is raining heavily outside and he supports the claim with the fact that he is soaking wet, and if this report does not conflict with our common knowledge about the world, it need not demand weighty evidence (though he may have been squirted with a hose or had a bucket of water dumped on him.) We can corroborate such claims by looking outside and/or receiving reports from other bystanders; and/or consulting a barometer. If, on the contrary, a person reports that it is raining pink fairies, skeptical inquirers request that his extraordinary account be corroborated by independent and impartial observers.

Seek Mundane Explanations

Few of us are free of superstitions or a fascination with Twilight Zones. I am surely not, and I'd hate to lose the pleasure of suspending disbelief—so long as I suspend it knowingly. Besides, we can't always distinguish the supernatural from natural phenomenon we don't yet understand. (Fax machines, like radio waves, seem magical to me.) But we should, at least, seek relatively mundane explanations for miraculous phenomena, like reported landings of UFOs or weeping statues of saints, before assuming that the most fantastic explanations are true.

Wendy Kaminer, *Sleeping with Extra-Terrestrials*, 1999.

Psychologist Elizabeth Loftus of the University of Washington (Fellow of CSICOP and a speaker at its 1994 convention) has performed numerous experiments to demonstrate the often fallible and deceptive character of memory. She found that many bystanders at a robbery or accident often offer conflicting reports, especially where the incident is emotionally charged. This tendency to misperceive may be compounded when someone claims to have seen a statue of the Virgin Mary weep or a miraculous cure by a faith healer. Not only must the report of an observer be carefully analyzed, but the interpretation that is placed upon it must be evaluated. Thus skeptical inquirers ask that wherever possible there be two or more witnesses to an event, that these witnesses be careful observers, and that what they have said can be independently corroborated. Reports of UFO visitations are common throughout the world, and these reports often come in waves, often depending on sensationalistic media exploitation. The investigator asks, What did these people really see? and Can these interpretations be verified? Skeptical inquirers have sought to provide prosaic explanations for unidentified flying objects, which are often identified as planets, meteors, weather balloons, terrestrial rockets, aircraft, or other phenomena.

Claims and Evidence

Extraordinary claims need extraordinary evidence: This principle has been adduced for anomalous accounts. If it is the case that a paranormal event, if confirmed, would overthrow the known laws of science, then one would need abundant evidence to accept it. The evidence must not be skimpy or haphazard, but so strong that its denial would require more credulity than its acceptance. The claim has been made that psychokinesis is genuine, that the mind can move matter without an intervening physical object or material force; or that precognitive events can be known before they happen. Helmut Schmidt has claimed experimental evidence that persons in the present can retrogressively affect past events in a random generator. This unusual anomaly would seem to violate the laws of physics, and/or it would require that physics be revised to account for it. We would need several lines of independent replication before we can accept the claim. . . .

Fraud: The resort to fraud is notorious in human affairs, including cases in orthodox science (for example, the Piltdown Man hoax). It is especially widespread in the paranormal area. Many mediums and psychics have been found cheating. Although some of the deception might be inadvertent, considerable intentional trickery has been uncovered. It is thus important that every precaution against deception be used. In the design of an experiment, safeguards ought to be built in so that the subjects under study cannot fudge the data, whether inadvertently or intentionally. . . .

Experimenter bias: The role of unconscious bias by an experimenter poses a problem in virtually all fields of science. Those who propose a theory are often not the best or most competent judges of the evidential basis in support of it. Experimenter bias may be conscious or unconscious. It may creep in by inadvertent sensory leakage or in assessment techniques. A good case is Michel Gauquelin, who was hailed by many as the founder of a new science of "astrobiology." Gauquelin claimed to have found a correlation between planetary configurations and professional achievement. He said that when Mars was in certain portions of the sky (key sectors 1 and 4) there was a tendency for greater sports champions to be born. There is considerable evidence that Gauquelin selected his sample based on prior knowledge of whether they were born with Mars in key sectors. Hence the effect found was due less to any Mars Effect than to Gauquelin's biased samples. Independent scientific inquiries were unable to replicate the efforts. . . .

The Hunger for Magic and Miracles

Magical thinking: Many skeptical inquirers have been puzzled by the ready tendency of many human beings to resort to magical thinking, i.e., to accept without sufficient evidence contracausal explanations. This includes the capacity for adopting paranormal interpretations and/or reading into nature occult forces. There is a tendency to attribute to some individuals miraculous powers. Historically, this applies to the prophets who claim to have had revelations from on high and to be endowed with supernatural abilities. This also applies to gurus, shamans, medicine men, psychics, and faith healers—who are believed to be possessed of magical powers. The person who resorts to magical thinking is more likely to accept the occult and/or psychic explanation without critical skepticism. The miracle worker is taken as an authority and the facts are stretched to validate the healing claim.

Psychological interpretations of the paranormal: Many skeptical inquirers maintain that the key to understanding paranormal phenomena is in human psychology and human nature. This has many dimensions: being amenable to suggestibility, being fantasy-prone, given to magical thinking, and having the general tendency to allow one's personal propensities, desires, and hopes to color the data. Ray Hyman has demonstrated the power of "cold reading" and how many people are taken in by it. But this can be generalized to many other paranormal fields.

The popularity of astrological horoscopes provides considerable support for a psychological interpretation. There is little or no evidence to support astrology, and it has failed virtually all the tests adduced to validate it. All efforts to find a statistical correlation between the moment and place of birth and the position of the heavenly bodies have had negative results. Yet many people claim that astrological sun signs and horoscopes are true. For the skeptic the more likely explanation is that truth is in the eye of the beholder. For the palm reader, astrologer, or psychic is often so general in his reading that his diagnoses and prognostications are stretched by the subject so that they are personally validated. Thus, in my view the key to the paranormal is that it is within the *eye of the beholder.* This is what I have labeled the "stretched-sock syndrome," for they can be stretched to fit any feet.

The transcendental temptation: Why is this so? I have postulated a "transcendental temptation" in human culture and human nature as a possible explanation for the tendency to accept a paranormal or occult universe. This perhaps has its roots in the long evolutionary history of the species and it may have even a genetic basis. Some, such as E.O. Wilson, have claimed sociobiological roots for religiosity, though many skeptics have criticized this theory as not being sufficiently tested. John Schumaker, an Australian psychologist, believes that some illusions are necessary for sanity, and that "the corruption of reality" is an essential ingredient of mental health. To face death or existential nothingness, he said, is difficult for most people, and so they achieve consolation by reading hidden meanings into nature, including belief in the afterlife or the ability to communicate with dead persons. The same explanation can be applied to many other areas of the paranormal. Gullibility is thus fed by the hunger for transcendence.

Hypnosis: One topic that has aroused considerable skeptical controversy concerns the reliability of hypnosis as a source of knowledge. Is hypnosis a special "trance state" induced in a subject, or is he or she simply acting out the suggestions of the hypnotist? It is clear that hypnosis is a useful technique in many areas of practice. It does have its pitfalls, however, concerning a whole range of paranormal phenomena, allegedly verified by hypnotic regression. This is the case in regard to "past-life regressions" used by some researchers as evidence for reincarnation. Budd Hopkins,

David Jacobs, and John Mack have introduced hypnotic regressions as evidence for abductions by alien beings, who are allegedly engaged in sexual or genetic experiments. Skeptics have argued that a more likely explanation for such bizarre tales is that the evidence is contaminated by the hypnotherapist, who, using suggestion, tends to implant the ideas in a person and/or assists in conjuring fantasies. The skeptic maintains that we need not postulate prior lives or extraterrestrial abductions in the paranormal realm, for there are still other possible alternative explanations. . . .

Given the tendency for "magical thinking," the "transcendental temptation," and "gullibility," skeptics have their work cut out for them. We cannot silently steal away once we have investigated and debunked an outrageous claim. There will always be a need for skeptical inquiry in society. Not only do the old myths crop up to entice a new generation and need responses, but new, often more fanciful claims may be introduced and become fashionable. Thus, I submit that there is a continuing need for skeptical inquiry, and skeptics will always serve as the gadflies of society. Standing in the wings of the theatre of life, unable to accept the prevailing nonsense on stage, the role of skeptics is to keep alive the spirit of free inquiry and to ask probing questions—even if those they criticize are deeply offended, and/or in spite of the calumny that may descend upon the skeptics for their criticisms.

"Where unorthodox claims persist for a long time, as, say, with psychic phenomena, [the] appeal to science fails to settle the matter."

Paranormal Phenomena Should Be Approached with an Open Mind

Henry H. Bauer

Scientific knowledge is not always reliable or correct and should not necessarily be depended on to explain paranormal phenomena, contends Henry H. Bauer in the following viewpoint. While science is a valuable tool, it may not reveal the truth about unusual events that defy logic or leave no recordable evidence. Psychic phenomena, for example, may be better investigated through psychological or spiritual knowledge rather than through purely scientific methods, Bauer points out. Investigators who want to be open to the possibility of discovering something new should recognize the value of knowledge systems other than science. Bauer, a former chemistry professor, is the author of *Science or Pseudoscience: Magnetic Healing, Psychic Phenomena, and Other Heterodoxies*, from which this viewpoint is excerpted.

As you read, consider the following questions:
1. In Bauer's opinion, what current arguments among experts reveal the limitations of scientific knowledge?
2. What is scientism, according to the author?
3. When is science at its best, in Bauer's view?

"Warm water freezes faster than cold," he alleged. He'd heard it, more or less accepted it, but never bothered to test it. Testing was easy enough. The claim proved to be wrong—as I had asserted it *must* be, for on the way to freezing, the warm water would first have to become cold, and that takes (extra) time.

"Eggs can be stood on end at the time of the equinox," one of my students told me. Not only had he heard that, he'd actually tried it and found it to be true. To prove it he brought photos taken at equinox time. "Could have been glue on the egg," I responded. To combat my skepticism, at the next equinox he brought a couple of eggs to class and demonstrated. For the next week or two, my family and I were much engaged in trying to stand eggs on end. We found that, given some persistence, nearly any egg can be stood on its larger end, equinox or not. That student had tested the claim, but he had not tested all of the claim; he had not done control experiments at other times than the equinox.

"Police radar can't pick up your car if you put aluminum foil in the hubcaps," other students informed me; and "You can beat a breathalyzer test by putting a copper penny under your tongue." Those claims were not so easily testable, so I called the state police laboratory for help. Technicians there were familiar with both claims and assured me that they are not valid.

The faster you go, the slower time passes and the heavier you get. Nothing in our everyday experience supports that claim. Yet, our best minds assure us, it is so and we should all believe it, though the effect is appreciable only at speeds that submicroscopic particles but not human beings can experience.

Nuclear fusion can be made to generate energy in a test tube at ordinary temperatures, by using palladium electrodes to pass electricity through "heavy" water. Some very competent people believe that. Some equally competent people dispute it.

There's a similar division of expert opinion over whether we're experiencing global warming because of the fossil fuels we've been burning; whether we've finally discovered the first planet outside our own solar system; whether we shall soon be able to make measurements of gravity waves; and a host of other scientific subjects.

Some people can predict the future. Some people can make contact with deceased loved ones. Some people have been abducted by aliens in UFOs and physically examined before being returned home. Those and many similar claims are made by intelligent people of considerable accomplishment. The same claims are dismissed as superstition or pseudoscience by other intelligent people of considerable accomplishment.

Whom and What Should People Believe?

Which authorities or experts are we to believe? Is it possible to find out whether such a claim is true or not? Is there at least some way to form a reasonable opinion?

If scientific knowledge were the only knowledge important to human beings—which it is not—then one could simply turn to science for guidance on what to believe.

If scientific knowledge were always correct—which it is not—then one would know what to believe at least on those matters with which science concerns itself.

If science were easily defined—which it is not—then it would also be easy to know when claimed knowledge is *pseudo*science rather than the real thing.

But as things stand, there is available no quick or easy guidance about what to believe, not only on the many matters over which apparently competent people differ but also over some where the experts seem to be in agreement. At times we do well to believe what we're told; at other times we had better not. Sometimes there's no better guide than the experience of what you've seen for yourself; at other times your eyes deceive you. We should be open to new ideas—but on the other hand we should always be skeptical and critical before accepting a new idea, for old beliefs are often well tested by experience whereas new ones may just be untested hunches. It's good to see the whole picture, to be holistic, to be interdisciplinary—but on the other hand, in many fields progress requires concentration on ultraspecialized techniques, theories, and facts.

One of the most pervasive generalities encountered in arguments over beliefs is that one ought to turn to science, or to the scientific method, to get a reliable answer. But many bits of erstwhile science turn out to be wrong; and some things that are true don't need to be and can't be scientifically proved, for example, that I love my daughters, and indeed science has nothing useful to say about such things.

The success of science over the last few centuries has been so impressive that we've come to equate science globally with truth. So when there are arguments about extrasensory perception or astrology or the like, it seems natural to ask what science has to say about it. It also seems to offer a desirable shortcut: instead of arguing directly over the particular evidence, we just invoke the authority of science. But where unorthodox claims persist for a long time, as, say, with psychic phenomena, this appeal to science fails to settle the matter. Instead of a shortcut, it turns out to be a distraction, a red herring. We argue over whether or not extrasensory perception or the like is science instead of whether or not it happens.

Knowledge fights are really about beliefs. It seems natural to presume that the things we believe are in fact true; indeed we imagine that we believe them *because* they're true. But of course that's not always the case—if it were, disagreements might be rare, whereas in fact they're commonplace. Arguing over whether or not something is "science," whether or not it is "pseudoscience," often is an attempt to enlist science's supposedly objective knowledge in support of personal beliefs. . . .

"Pseudoscience" Versus Science?

Positing "pseudoscience" in contrast to science implies that one is the opposite of the other. Yet the subjects so often called pseudoscience seem to develop in parallel with advances in mainstream science; according to Thomas Leahey and Grace Leahey "it is psychology that spawns pseudosciences and therapeutic cults."

The attempt to distinguish science from pseudoscience is not itself a matter of natural science. Therefore we shouldn't expect to find generalizations as precise as scientific laws, or even clearly right-or-wrong answers, about whether a given claim is or isn't science. We have to settle for generalizations that are less than universal, that apply in many but not all cases of any given sort. To acquire judgment, when to believe and when not to, when to accept what one sees and when not to, one needs both good generalizations and also the benefit of experience of actual cases, especially those where people went wrong, as a guide to when exceptions to those good generalizations may be warranted.

One of my goals is to identify useful generalizations about the seeking of new knowledge and to test them against particular instances of knowledge fights. My concern is especially with those controversies that are largely outside the mainstream of science: about psychic phenomena, UFOs, or Loch Ness monsters ("Nessies")—anomalous or anomalist or anomalistic phenomena. . . .

The Nature of Anomalistics

Science studies the natural world. Extrasensory perception may seem to be a claimed phenomenon of the physical world and therefore appropriately subject to the authority of science; yet actually it is about human behavior and as such a matter for psychology at least as much as for physics. Quite generally in anomalistics, at stake are matters of human behavior and human beliefs, regarding which the natural sciences have nothing much to say whereas the social sciences (and theology) do. Consider astrology: it is about how the cosmos influences our lives. Astrology doesn't argue against the laws of gravity or electromagnetism; it doesn't claim to be able to calculate orbits better than astronomy can. The appeal of astrology is its concern with human fate. That astronomy cannot make sense of astrology's procedures, that to astronomers the astrologers may be scientific illiterates, is quite beside the point. If astrology is opposed to any accepted knowledge, it is to psychological, religious, or spiritual knowledge more than to astronomical.

Again, the fascination that UFOs exert is not because they perhaps reveal ways of traveling faster than we now imagine possible but because they touch an age-old question: Are humans the only conscious, intelligent beings in the whole cosmos? Alchemy, nowadays a standard example of pseudoscience, is often referred to as though it had been merely a superseded premodern chemistry, but it was actually a whole system or worldview much like astrology or magic, in which properties of nature and of humans were intimately and meaningfully connected.

What Science Must Concede

The scientific establishment [must be] prepared to concede that unreason might well have its reasons. Science must admit its catastrophes as well as its triumphs; it must plumb the darkness that shadows Enlightenment reason. Science must also concede that ambiguity and mystery—for which popular mysticism is roundly decried—is often to be found at the very core of its frontier disciplines. And, finally, science will have to accept that it is always shaped by culture and society—from its theorems to its funding programmes—and that a radically different society and culture may demand a radically different scientific practice.

Pat Kane, *New Statesman (1996)*, August 23, 1996.

Folklore about "moon madness"—*lunacy*—would have it that humans tend to behave peculiarly when the moon is full. Anomalistics more than science would take that claim seriously. Assume that statistical evidence of such an effect is offered. It might be because the moon exerts a physical influence as it does on the tides; or, perhaps human behavior is influenced by the phases of the moon just because folklore has convinced some number of people that it is so, and they behave accordingly—in a similar fashion as Australian aborigines tend to die when they find themselves the victims of bone pointing. [Bone pointing is a form of ritual execution in Aboriginal cultures. A hexed bone is pointed at an intended victim, eventually resulting in his or her death even though the weapon does not come in physical contact with the victim.] So claims of this sort cannot be validly dismissed by insisting that the moon could not possibly influence human behavior because it is so far away that its gravitational or other physical effect could not be discernible by individuals.

It is not always easy in natural science to prove that something is *not* so; in social science, it's even harder. Even if some number of studies show no clearly significant statistical evidence for a moon-phase influence on human behavior, such an influence might nevertheless be strongly evident with some people, just as bone pointing may effectively kill Australian aborigines but not Freudian psychoanalysts. On this point, anomalistics shares dilemmas with medicine: statistical studies showing that some new drug has no obvious side-effects might well miss its effect on, say, pregnant women, as happened with thalidomide. No study can look specifically at every possible subset of human beings that might be affected in some idiosyncratic manner.

Scientism

Claims about moon-phase effects and a host of other such matters are typically dismissed by reference to what natural science supposedly knows, revealing the extent to which some people—science groupies and dedicated debunkers of heretical claims—look to natural science as the supreme arbiter of truth. This *scientistic* attitude becomes insupportable when one stops to think about it. Nevertheless, at the level of implicit belief that shapes so much individual and public action, scientism is the prevalent faith of the modern age; the manner in which we talk about "science" in everyday discourse and the metaphors from science that we draw on illustrate that. Just consider how often we are told that *scientific* tests—not just any old tests—have proven something to be true.

A few hundred years ago, before the Scientific Revolution and the Enlightenment, questions of truth were the concern of the church. Nowadays science has superseded the church as universal knowledge authority. Science has itself become a sort of church, and scientists are in that sense also priests. Science nowadays like the church in earlier centuries feels responsible for the intellectual orderliness of society. Thus pseudoscience is *heretical* belief—not merely wrong but an actual danger to the proper functioning of society and the welfare of humankind. The passion that authority always vents against heresy is directed nowadays in the name of science against pseudoscience.

So framing issues about extrasensory perception and the like as science versus pseudoscience is quite natural to our times; yet it misses the most important point, that the appeal of much so-called pseudoscience is on psychological or quasi-religious grounds and not on purely intellectual or scientific ones. Calling something pseudoscience implies that it isn't science but ought to be. Yet why should the study of psychic phenomena resemble the work of physics or chemistry?

The Limits of Textbook Science

It isn't commonly remembered that scientific knowledge varies from highly reliable to highly unreliable. The most reliable is so in large part because it has worked well for a long time without contradiction; but such *textbook* science is a far cry from the *frontier* science that represents research in progress or the latest breakthroughs trumpeted to and by the media.

The interesting knowledge fights are over new knowledge, frontier stuff. We don't worry much about such pseudo-sciences as flat-earth theory or alchemy, disproof of which by science has long been possible through convincing demonstrations performable at will. What produces tension are the issues for which science presently lacks resounding answers.

Ask, for example, "What is the real identity of Unidentified Flying Objects?" and science is said to answer, "More than 90 percent of reports have been explained as misidentifications of Venus, Earth satellites, rockets, meteors, helicopters, marsh gas, lenticular clouds, radar anomalies, and so on. In maybe 5 or 10 percent of the cases, we don't have enough information; but if we did, no doubt the same sort of explanation would apply." That's typical of the sort of answer that those who claim to speak for science like to offer: based on solid, long-attested textbook knowledge, using the most conservative extrapolation from it, in the faith that current mysteries will eventually prove to be explainable by already understood laws.

But that is not a very good answer to offer someone who sees in current mysteries a possible opportunity to discover new laws.

Ask, "How does a placebo work?" The answer you get from science will be no better than what you hear from a practitioner of alternative medicine about acupuncture or therapeutic touch; indeed, it may well seem not as good. In both instances, "explanations" are being offered for things that actually we do not understand.

Science is at its best when it is on the most certain ground. Confronted with what is not yet properly understood, those who claim to speak for science are reluctant to admit ignorance, and therefore their answers often discount or evade. So controversy ensues on the frontiers and fringes of science. It's only natural, of course, that the bitterest controversies involve the most uncertain matters. But those are also the ones that arouse the greatest interest.

Periodical Bibliography

The following articles have been selected to supplement the diverse views presented in this chapter.

Wayne R. Anderson   "Why Would People Not Believe Weird Things?" *Skeptical Inquirer*, September/October 1998.

Bufo Calvin   "Power Thinking and the Paranormal," *Fate*, March 1998.

John Derbyshire   "Stars Above!: Astrology Is Ascending, Which Is Bad News," *National Review*, July 9, 2001.

John David Ebert   "From Cellular Aging to the Physics of Angels: A Conversation with Rupert Sheldrake," *The Quest*, Spring 1998.

Kendrick Frazier   "From the Editor's Seat: Thoughts on Science and Skepticism in the Twenty-First Century," *Skeptical Inquirer*, July 2001.

Fulvia Gloria-Bottini   "Does Birthdate Determine Destiny?" *Chemistry and Industry*, July 1, 1996.

Dyan Machan   "Bah, Humbug!: Paul Kurtz Offers a Message for Which There Is Scant Demand These Days—The Deflating Truth About UFOs, Reincarnation and Alternative Medicine," *Forbes*, March 6, 2000.

David Perlman   "Sideshows of Science: As Knowledge Expands, So Do the Ranks of Believers in Fakery," *San Francisco Chronicle*, January 8, 2001.

James Randi   "Million Dollar Madness," *Skeptic* (Altadena, CA), Fall 1999.

Jack Raso and Samuel Homola   "Pseudoscience and Antiscience in Alternative Medicine," *Priorities for Health*, Volume 12, Number 4, 2000.

Ted Roach   "The Physics of Space, Time, and Flying Saucers," *NEXUS*, February/March 1998.

Glenn G. Sparks   "Paranormal Depictions in the Media: How Do They Affect What People Believe?" *Skeptical Inquirer*, July/August 1998.

Glenn G. Sparks et al.   "Does Television News About UFOs Affect Viewers' UFO Beliefs? An Experimental Investigation," *Communication Quarterly*, Summer 1998.

Tikkun   "Spirit and Health: An Interview with Larry Dossey," March/April 2000.

Is There Proof That Paranormal Phenomena Exist?

Chapter Preface

One of the main challenges for researchers attempting to prove the existence of the paranormal is to develop an experiment that can be repeated and verified by other scientists. For most of the twentieth century, the most serious criticism of parapsychology—the study of psychic phenomena, often referred to as *psi*—was that it had not yielded any reliable display of psychic ability that could be replicated by other investigators. In the mid-1970s, however, several researchers adapted a technique from experimental psychology that promised to provide a repeatable demonstration: the ganzfeld procedure.

In the ganzfeld experiment, a person whose psychic ability is being tested (the receiver) is isolated in a room and subjected to a mild form of sensory deprivation. In a separate room, a sender concentrates on a randomly selected video clip or photograph. After thirty minutes, the receiver is shown four pictures or video clips and is asked to choose the one that most closely fits the mental images he or she perceived while isolated. According to experimenters, the receiver would have a 25 percent chance of guessing the correct picture or video clip. If over a sufficient number of experiments a receiver picks the correct target more than 30 percent of the time, then extrasensory perception (ESP) has been demonstrated.

In 1994, Cornell University psychologist Daryl Bem and University of Edinburgh parapsychologist Charles Honorton published a metanalysis (a statistical technique that allows researchers to pool results across a number of studies) of forty-two ganzfeld studies that appeared to provide convincing proof of the existence of ESP. According to their data, receivers achieved an average "hit" rate of 35 percent. Bem points out that "the odds against getting a 35 percent hit rate across that many studies by chance are greater than a billion to one." Moreover, Bem and Honorton reported that they discovered several predictors of psychic ability. Subjects who were artistic, extroverted, and had previously studied a mental discipline such as meditation obtained especially high hit rates.

Many regarded Bem and Honorton's findings as providing the most compelling evidence ever of the existence of ESP. However, in 1999, researchers Julie Milton and Richard Wiseman published an updated metanalysis of thirty recent ganzfeld studies not reviewed by Bem and Honorton. Milton and Wiseman failed to replicate the findings of the earlier metanalysis, reporting the same results that would have been achieved by random chance. "Seemingly replicable parapsychological findings have again proven to be disconcertingly elusive, and the experimental ESP literature has again proven to be consistently inconsistent," contends Emory University psychologist Scott Littlefield.

Interestingly, Milton and Wiseman *did* find that subjects who had practiced a mental discipline scored higher than average on the ganzfeld tests. Unless additional experiments back up their findings, however, skeptics will continue to maintain that the existence of ESP has not been proven.

The search for proof of the paranormal involves intriguing experiments and methods of data collection. The authors in the following chapter discuss whether investigators have uncovered any conclusive evidence that confirms the existence of ghosts, psychic ability, and alien spacecraft.

> *"Among the most common phenomena found at ghost research sites are apparently floating, circular or diamond-shaped objects called 'orbs,' which have been captured in many photographs."*

Some Evidence Indicates the Existence of Ghosts

J. Michael Krivyanski

In the following viewpoint, J. Michael Krivyanski discusses the techniques that researchers of the paranormal use to investigate ghost phenomena. In addition to collecting historical information about sites in question, writes Krivyanski, ghost investigators use various cameras, electromagnetic field detectors, thermal scanners, and tape recorders to gather data associated with a haunting. According to the author, ghost researchers have recorded unusual magnetic fields, "cold spots" in rooms, unexplained sounds, floating orbs, and other anomalous phenomena at haunted locales that seem to provide evidence that ghosts exist. Krivyanski is a freelance writer residing in Allison Park, Pennsylvania.

As you read, consider the following questions:

1. According to researcher Sherry Higgins, quoted by the author, what are some examples of electronic voice phenomena?
2. What is ecto-mist, according to Krivyanski?
3. Why is it difficult for ghost investigators to receive funding for their research, in the author's opinion?

Excerpted from "Probing the Phenomena Called Ghosts," by J. Michael Krivyanski, *World & I*, August 2001. Copyright © 2001 by News World Communications, Inc. Reprinted with permission.

Persistent and puzzling reports of spectral presences have fostered the emergence of independent, mostly amateur investigators who use scientific instruments to capture evidence of anomalous energy dynamics in apparently unoccupied places.

While on their way to a prescreened site, a small group of investigators carefully review all the background work they've done. The history of the area has been well documented, and people who've had relevant experiences there have been interviewed.

Once at the site, the investigators explore as they make notes. Based on what they've learned previously and what they observe, they'll decide where to set up their equipment.

A few places will be good for the infrared video cameras, which will be connected by cables to television monitors at a central location. Other locations will be selected for digital sound recording equipment. While some of them will observe what happens on the monitors, others will be taking digital photos at different places around the site. Some will measure magnetic fields with electromagnetic field (EMF) detectors. Others may use thermal scanners to measure any temperature changes. The team members are busy taking pictures and readings the entire time they're at the location.

Their type of work doesn't receive any funding or grants. These researchers are extremely dedicated to what they do, surviving on their own investments and an occasional donation.

The strong desire to use scientific instruments to probe reported ghost phenomena has drawn together these five people from California, Pennsylvania. Similar investigations are conducted by small groups or individuals all around the country and in many parts of the world.

Their group, the Mon Valley Ghost Research Society (MVGRS), conducts roughly 3–5 research site visits a month. A complete investigation of one site includes 1–4 visits, depending on the proximity and activity. The team leader, Rene Kruse, holds a Ph.D. in industrial engineering from Texas A&M University and is a full professor in the applied engineering department at California University in Pennsylvania, where she's been working for the past 12 years. Other team members are homemakers Sherri Higgins and Linda Davis; David Ross, a plastics manufacturing plant supervisor; and Edgar Harris, a retired expert on local history.

Deluded or Foresightful?

The notion of investigating spectral phenomena using scientific instruments may sound goofy or even egregiously unsound to those who assume that all references to ghosts are products of the imagination. Yet ghost investigators are drawn to persist in their efforts. Their instruments regularly record anomalous heat or cold, light or infrared radiation, magnetic fields or sound at sites where people have reported activity that is often characterized as the appearance of a ghost or a spirit from bygone times. Dismissed by practically all scientists, ghost investigators exchange results and ideas among themselves, aided greatly by the Internet. Are they all deluded, or are they pioneering a new frontier of scientific investigation?

Kruse, a mother of four who in her day job teaches engineering students the nuts and bolts of the science they need to know, is not easily confused about measurements of magnetic fields, sounds, temperatures, and reflective bodies.

"I started doing [ghost research] about 25 years ago," says Kruse, "and have been doing active investigations in varying degrees for about the past 10 years. In the beginning most of my investigations were conducted out of state, because I wasn't sure how my colleagues and neighbors would perceive my avocation. By now, everyone is very warm and excited about my research. Every time I'm on a TV show I get a flood of e-mail from people I know and work with. Everyone, including students, has been extremely positive about it.

"I met Sherri and Dave at a ghost conference, and we started working together. Sherri and I were doing several experiments in a local cemetery of which Edgar was the cemetery president. He came along with us [on an investigation] and got hooked. Linda lived at the site of one of my earlier investigations. After a couple of investigations together, we decided that we should somewhat formalize our group and gave ourselves a name. There's also been a sizable monetary investment by most of us," says Kruse.

Investigating Ghost Activity

They have decided to limit their team to five since the members have taken on complementary functions that cover the essential aspects of an investigation. They feel that if the group grows, they'll cease to be efficient.

MVGRS has presented the results of its investigations to historical societies, library groups, and civic groups. Its members would welcome the opportunity to present their results to the scientific community but have no appropriate bridges into that community at this time.

When asked to investigate a site, the MVGRS team usually begins by collecting information. They talk to all those who have had anomalous experiences at the location and are particularly interested in such questions as "Who died there? What was unique about the people who died there? What were the circumstances of their deaths?" Researchers find a definite correlation between the type of activity that currently occurs at a site and whatever happened there earlier. Knowing these things helps them decide how best to conduct the research.

Electrical Readings

Magnetometers measure magnetic fields given off by a variety of sources, including technology in the house. There is a general background reading in the location, and readings will increase when you bring the magnetometer near VCRs, digital alarm clocks, electrical outlets, or anything else that has an electric current running through it Ghost investigators must take both the background reading and the location of electronic devices into consideration when sweeping a house with a magnetometer.

Considering that, it's interesting to observe consistently higher—sometimes much higher—magnetic readings in spots where people have witnessed haunting phenomena. These local magnetic fields persist even with all household power turned off.

Loyd Auerbach, *Fate*, February 1999.

During an investigation, the team collects photographic evidence using infrared [IR] video cameras, 35-millimeter still cameras (usually with a flash), and visual digital cameras.

They also use video cameras to tape witnesses of the suspected hauntings to provide a good record of the interview, as body language can often provide insights into the reliability of a report.

Anomalous magnetic fields are often associated with sites where ghost activity has been reported. Thus, electromagnetic field (EMF) detectors for detecting anomalous magnetic fields are standard equipment. The EMF meter filters out magnetic fields produced by alternating currents in wires to read natural magnetic field levels. "A normal, ambient magnetic field is on the order of 0–3 milligauss," says Kruse. "In the vicinity of electrical appliances (like a refrigerator or TV), the magnetic fields can reach abnormal levels. Readings associated with ghosts are often above 8 milligauss, although I have seen one registering as high as 150 milligauss, which is the highest reading on the meter."

Cold Spots and Electronic Voices

One common type of anomaly encountered by those who probe the phenomena called ghosts is "cold spots," zones in the air that are unexplainably cold, sometimes many degrees lower than the rest of the room. In addition to directly detecting cold air on their skin, the MVGRS team employs laser digital thermal scanners to monitor surface temperatures. Other ghost researchers also use digital thermal probes that give instant readouts of air temperature where the probe is placed. This enables the user to better read cold spots. In addition, thermal-imaging scopes and cameras allow the researchers to see photographic images based on thermal patterns.

Some cold spots move and some simply vanish. There aren't many theories concerning them, but cold spots have been written about for hundreds of years. "The reason cold spots have been written about for so long is that they may be detected by anyone and without any sophisticated equipment," says Kruse. "Cold spots may be considered a form of manifestation, such as visual, auditory, olfactory, or tactile. Sometimes, an entire room might get cold or a fairly well-defined area with detectable parameters within a room. Occasionally, there will be reports of a room in a house that the residents just can't get to warm up, regardless of the season. Cold spots also are found outside. Our group only considers a cold spot significant if we measure a drop in temperature of 15 degrees F or greater."

For recording unexplained sounds, ghost research groups use regular magnetic audiotape recorders and minidisc digital recorders. They also record their own verbal reports of what occurs during the investigation. In addition, the machines sometimes record unexplained voices in what is called electronic voice phenomena (EVP).

Sherri Higgins is the team member who concentrates on EVP.

"Most of the time, when we do record an EVP," says Higgins, "it is a comment to a conversation the investigators are having at the time with the partners. The voice is always distinguishable as man, woman, or child. Or animal. For example: my first time out years ago, I was walking through a local cemetery when my camera stopped working. I kept taping with a portable recorder in my friend's pocket. We casually chatted about the beauty of the cemetery. Later when we listened to the recording, after I said "What a peaceful area," an eerie whisper of a clearly recognizable female voice said "peaceful." We almost fell over, and the goosebumps rose on our arms. We played that tape over about 20 times.

"The animal sound I've recorded was a horse trotting across Sachs Bridge in Gettysburg, Pennsylvania. You can actually hear the horseshoes clomping across the wooden bridge (about 10 times), then it fades away. This was captured on the audio of the video recorder."

Orbs

Among the most common phenomena found at ghost research sites are apparently floating, circular or diamond-shaped objects called "orbs," which have been captured in many photographs. Video cameras have shown their images floating across the screen, while digital and 35-millimeter cameras have photographed orbs larger than basketballs or as small as a postcard.

Many theories attempt to explain them. "Although skeptics want to dismiss the orb photos as being caused by something like dust specks on the camera lens or a flaw in the film," says Kruse, "these explanations are clearly inadequate. When we pick up similar images from different cameras, and those images are recorded in sites corresponding to anomalous magnetic fields or cold spots, then, we say, it is reasonable to assert that something more than normal is happening here.

"Many of us in the field," says Kruse, "believe that the orbs are a manifestation of some kind of spirit energy. Others think in terms of magnetic fields reacting to elements in the ground.

"An example of evidence that we, the MVGRS, have witnessed and recorded happened in a private home in southwestern Pennsylvania. The household contained two parents and three children. The youngest, a four-year-old boy, had experienced night terrors at a younger age. The mother felt that a ghost was disturbing the sleep of her young son. She had convinced herself that her son was waking up crying every night because a ghost was disturbing him.

"We set up an overlapping video format to monitor her son while he slept. His room had two doors, one to the bathroom and, on an adjacent wall, a door opening onto a stairway. We set one IR [infrared] video camera in the bathroom aimed at the son while he slept. The other video camera was placed at the bottom of the stairway, pointing up at the boy's door. Both cameras were hardwired to monitors set up in the living room with five people watching. Two people remained upstairs in another bedroom.

"At one point, the boy awoke from a sound sleep, started to cry loudly, and sat up in bed crying and rubbing his eyes. After several seconds of this, the monitor aimed at the boy's door recorded several orbs moving up the stairs and disappearing through the door. There, the camera trained on the boy picked up the orbs appearing on the other side of the door, inside the bedroom. They moved slowly over the boy, and he lay back down and went right back to sleep. It appeared that we had detected a spirit/ghost that had comforted or calmed the boy, rather than awakened him. This was witnessed in real time by the people watching the monitors downstairs and the two witnesses upstairs.

"Are orbs more than a photographic anomaly? Recently, three members of the MVGRS were conducting an investigation in a prestigious museum and were experiencing (via IR video) heightened activity. One member watched for an orb to tell the other when to shoot a digital photo. This went on for quite some time. On 11 occasions during this experience, we were able to capture a digital photo of the same orb that we were seeing on the video screen. On one occasion, we saw three orbs moving along a wall on the video screen and caught all three in a single photo in the same spot in which they were viewed on video. Another factor is that there was a high-tech environmental air filtration system in place in the building [which greatly reduces dust specks in the air]," says Kruse.

Another common finding is called "ecto-mist." This is a white cloud that can appear, disappear, and reappear or even move from room to room. Images of ecto-mists have been captured, often by video recorders as well as still cameras. The theories on ecto-mists are similar to those about orbs. While some believe them to be spirit energy, others feel they're a result of magnetic fields being trapped within a confined area. Kruse knows of no experiments that have been conducted to prove or disprove the latter theory.

Challenging the Results

After they finish and return to their homes, the group members carefully analyze every moment of videotape, audiotape, and any notes they took. They then produce a report, giving a copy to the owners of the site and keeping one for themselves. They compare their findings for different sites and keep looking for more places to investigate.

"When we witness or record something that is new to us, or that we can't explain, we will do everything we can to determine if it has a natural explanation," says Kruse. "We do, in fact, try to disprove almost every anomaly that we record. This way, what we are left with is more reliable. Example: we investigated a house built in the late 1700s. This house was documented to have been on the underground railroad. The 'hiding room' was in the basement. It was completely underground, had walls made of limestone over one and a half feet thick, no windows, three walls backed by soil, and only one doorway.

"There was a room above it, with additional rooms extending beyond the walls of the hiding room in the basement. We set up a video camera in the doorway, shooting into the room, and left it recording for four hours. Five times during this period, in two groups of twos and one single time, a bright light would form on the wall to the right of the camera and rapidly shoot across the room to the left. We had never seen this phenomenon before but were very excited at the prospect of discovering something new. We went back to the house and set everything up the same way and then tried everything we could to re-create the event naturally.

"We eventually found that there was a small hole in the baseboard of a room upstairs, not the room directly above the hiding room but the one to the right of the room directly above. When someone swept the baseboard of the wall above and the light hit the small hole, it shot light through the room, which had an amplified effect on the IR camera. We had explained the cause of our mysterious shooting light. Our 'discovery' was exciting for a while, but we maintained our integrity. This was not the only example but one of many," says Kruse. . . .

The fact that there isn't ongoing research funded by grants to learn more about ghosts is not difficult to understand. Scientists have a pretty clear model of the way the world works, and phenomena associated with ghosts don't fit into that model. Furthermore, the fact that many who report ghost phenomena presume that ghosts are spirits of deceased humans explicitly defines the field as lying beyond the reach of science. Barring some major, unforeseen development, it seems likely that the phenomena called ghosts will remain on the margins of science for a long time.

"To date there is no credible scientific evidence that inns—or any other sites—are inhabited by spirits of the dead."

There Is No Evidence That Ghosts Exist

Joe Nickell

Joe Nickell, author of numerous investigative books, is the senior research fellow of the Committee for the Scientific Investigation of Claims of the Paranormal. In the following viewpoint, Nickell maintains that so-called hauntings are typically the result of ordinary occurrences such as waking dreams, sleep paralysis, rumors, fantasies, or hoaxes. In addition, normal physical phenomena such as noises or pieces of lint in the eyes can trigger mental images that some people perceive as ghosts, the author explains. Popular tales about haunted places can influence the minds of imaginative people, and fantasy-prone individuals often attribute an unexplained but ordinary event to a ghostly visitation. However, there is no scientific proof of the existence of ghosts, Nickell concludes.

As you read, consider the following questions:
1. What happens during waking dreams, according to Nickell?
2. According to the author, how can the ambiance of a place contribute to claims that it is haunted?
3. In what ways do professional "psychics" encourage belief in ghosts, according to Nickell?

Excerpted from "Haunted Inns: Tales of Spectral Ghosts," by Joe Nickell, *Skeptical Inquirer*, September 2000. Copyright © 2000 by The Committee for the Scientific Investigation of Claims of the Paranormal. Reprinted with permission.

I f testimonials in countless books and articles are to be believed, spending the night in a quaint old hotel might provide an encounter with an extra, ethereal visitor.

Over nearly thirty years of paranormal investigation, I
have had the opportunity to experience many "haunted"
sites. These have included burial places, like England's West
Kennet Long Barrow (where I failed to see the specter of a
"Druid priest" that allegedly attends the ancient tomb); religious sanctuaries, such as Christ Church Cathedral in Fred-
ericton, New Brunswick, Canada (where the apparition of
the first bishop's wife did not materialize); theaters, including the Lancaster (New York) Opera House (where a ghostly
"Lady in Lavender" was a no-show); houses, like the historic
residence of William Lyon Mackenzie in Toronto (where
ghostly footfalls on the stairs were actually those of real
people on a staircase next door); and other sites, notably
inns—the subject of this investigative roundup. (Most of the
inns cited—all personally investigated—included an overnight stay, staff interviews, background research, etc.)

Why haunted inns? Obviously, places open to the public
have more numerous and more varied visitors, and hence
more opportunities for ghostly experiences, than do private
dwellings and out-of-the-way sites. And inns—by which I
include hotels, motels, guesthouses, bed-and-breakfasts, and
other places that provide overnight lodging—offer much
more. They not only allow extended time periods for visitors
to have unusual experiences but also ensure that the guests
will be there during a range of states from alertness through
sleep. Almost predictably, sooner or later, someone will
awaken to an apparition at his or her bedside.

Waking Dreams

The experience is a common type of hallucination, known
popularly as a "waking dream," which takes place between
being fully asleep and fully awake. Such experiences typically
include bizarre imagery (bright lights or apparitions of
demons, ghosts, aliens, etc.) and/or auditory hallucinations.
"Sleep paralysis" may also occur, whereby there is an inability to move because the body is still in the sleep mode.

A good example of an obvious waking dream is reported

by "A.C." She was asleep on board the Queen Mary, the former ocean liner that, since 1971, has been permanently docked at Long Beach, California. As reported by Robert Wlodarski, Anne Nathan-Wlodarski, and Richard Senate in their 1995 book *A Guide to the Haunted Queen Mary*, the woman relates:

> I awoke from a deep sleep around midnight. I saw a figure walking near my daughter's sleeping bag toward the door. Thinking it was my sister, I called out. There was no answer. It was then that I noticed my sister was lying next to me. I sat up in bed and watched the person in white walk through the door!

Another example reported at the Hotel Queen Mary is credited to "H.V.":

> I was awakened from my sleep and observed the image of a person standing in front of my bed. There were no apparent physical features, but it appeared to be holding a flashlight, with a light shining out of it that was brighter than the form itself. I watched as the image swayed back and forth. When I called my roommate the image backed up. I called again and the vision backed up even further, toward the door. I reached for the light switch and tried to turn it on. The light switch seemed to spark and wouldn't turn on all the way. Finally, my roommate woke up; the light came on, and whatever it was, was gone. We slept with the TV on the rest of the night. It was a great experience, and I had a lot of fun!

Illusions and Mental Images

To be sure, not all sightings of ghostly figures are of the waking-dream variety, many in fact occurring during normal activity. Some are like the report of "J.M." who was at the Queen Mary's Purser's Desk when, he stated, "I caught a brief glimpse out of the corner of my eye, of someone or something moving," or like that of "P.T." who said, "I saw something move out of the corner of my eye . . . a brief glimpse of someone or something." Actually, the illusion that something is moving in the peripheral vision is quite common. The typical cause may be a "floater," a bit of drifting material in the eye's vitreous humour, although a twitching eyelid, or other occurrence is also possible.

Such an illusion or a different stimulus—a noise, a subjective feeling, etc.—might trigger, as in one experiencer aboard the Queen Mary, a mental image. In that case it was of a man wearing a blue mechanic's uniform—a "feeling" which left after a few moments. In certain especially imaginative individuals the mental image might be superimposed upon the visual scene, thus creating a seemingly apparitional event.

This may be the explanation for a frequently reported type of apparition that is seen momentarily and then vanishes when the percipient looks away for an instant. For example, a New Mexico hotel, La Posada de Santa Fe—which is allegedly haunted by the spirit of Julie Staab (1844–1896), wife of the original builder—offers no fewer than three sightings of this type. One was reported in 1979 by an employee who was cleaning one night. Although the place was deserted he looked up to see a translucent woman standing near a fireplace. Inexplicably, notes Robin Mead, author of *Haunted Hotels: A Guide to American and Canadian Inns and Their Ghosts*, he "returned to his cleaning," an act that . . . showed "remarkable composure." Then, "when he looked up again the figure had vanished." On another occasion a security guard showed less reserve when, seeing what he thought was Julie, "He turned and ran, and when he looked back, the figure had vanished." Yet again, a "beautifully dressed" Julie, reposing in an armchair, was seen by the hotel phone operator. However, "When she looked back at the chair a few seconds later, the ghost had vanished." Such reports suggest that the apparition is only a mental image that occurs in a kind of reverie.

Indeed, personal experience as well as research data demonstrates that ghostly perceptions often derive from daydreams or other altered states of consciousness. E. Haraldsson for instance specifically determined that apparitional sightings were linked to periods of reverie. As well, Andrew MacKenzie demonstrated that a third of the hallucinatory cases he studied occurred either just before or after sleep, or while the percipient was in a relaxed state or concentrating on some activity like reading, or was performing routine work. The association of apparitional experiences with a dream-like state was also reported by G.N.M. Terrell. He observed that apparitions of people invariably appear fully clothed and are frequently accompanied by objects, just as they are in dreams, because the clothing and other objects are required by the apparitional drama. The three La Posada encounters are consistent with all of these research observations. That the apparitions vanish when the observer's gaze is shifted could be explained by the hypothesis that the reverie is merely broken.

Whereas "waking-dream" type encounters are obviously more likely to be experienced by hotel guests rather than employees, the reverie or daydream type is often reported by the latter—as in all three of the La Posada examples, as well as some of the instances from the Queen Mary and elsewhere. Hotel staff performing routine chores may be particularly susceptible to this type of apparitional experience.

Selling Ghosts

The power of suggestion can help trigger ghostly encounters. According to noted psychologist and fellow ghost-buster Robert A. Baker, "We tend to see and hear those things we believe in." Even without the prompting that comes from an inn's reputation for being haunted, the mere ambiance of places with antique architecture and quaint decor can set the stage for spirits to debut. An example is Belhurst Castle, a turreted stone inn in Geneva, New York, whose high-ceilinged lobby is graced with wood paneling, a large fireplace, and a suit of armor to help conjure up romantic notions. Historic sites like Maine's Kennebunk Inn (expanded from a home built in 1799), the Farnsworth House in Gettysburg, Pennsylvania, (constructed in 1810 and its south side pockmarked with bullet holes from the Battle of Gettysburg), and even the more recent Hotel Boulderado in Boulder, Colorado (which opened on New Year's Day 1909 and boasts among its former guests Bat Masterson), offer the impress of history and legend. So does the Bardstown, Kentucky, Jailer's Inn, a bed-and-breakfast converted from the old Nelson County Jail (built in 1819), and, in Santa Fe, the historic adobe La Fonda Inn.

The influence of setting and mood on reports of phantoms is sometimes acknowledged even by those who approach the subject with great credulity, although they may interpret the linkage differently. Broadcaster Andrew Green, for example, in his 1995 treatise *Haunted Inns and Taverns*, says of some copies of English pubs in Europe, the United States, and elsewhere: "A few have reproduced the ambiance so successfully that ghostly manifestations, such as might be associated with a genuine article, have occurred there." Green opines that the "genial atmosphere" of such taverns attracts authentic English ghosts. He seems not to consider the possibility that the setting merely influences the imaginations of those making the reports.

The Amityville Hoax

America's most famous haunted house is located in Amityville, New York, where in 1974 a man murdered his parents and siblings. A year later the house was bought by a couple who soon claimed they were driven out by spooky events. But an investigation showed the events never transpired, and the murderer's lawyer confessed how, for money, he and the couple had "created this horror story over many bottles of wine."

Joe Nickell and Matt Nisbett, *Skeptical Inquirer*, July/August 1998.

In contrast is the knowing statement of ghost hunter Mason Winfield—referring to the allegedly haunted Holiday Inn at Grand Island, New York—that "The environment of the Inn is not the gloomy, historic sort that puts people in mind of spooks." As one who has spent an uneventful night in that resort hotel, indeed in its reputedly most-haunted room 422, I quite agree. But apparitions can occur anywhere. The Holiday Inn's child ghost "Tanya" apparently originated with an impressionable maid who was cleaning the fourth-floor room shortly after the hotel opened in 1973. The housekeeper suddenly glimpsed a little girl standing in the doorway and, startled, dropped a couple of drinking glasses. When she looked up again, the child was gone. As the maid tried to flee, it was reported, "somehow her cart trapped her in the room. She screamed." Her apparitional encounter seems consistent with the typical conditions we have already discussed: at the time, she was performing routine chores. As to the cart, most likely, flustered, she merely encountered it where she had left it, blocking her flight, and panicked.

Other sightings there—like that of a Canadian man who

awoke to see a little girl at the foot of his bed—were of the waking-dream variety. But why is it often a little girl (even if varyingly identified as age "five or six" or "about age 10")? Those knowing about "Tanya" before their sighting may thus be influenced, while those who do not may, in light of subsequent statements or leading questions from those to whom they report an incident, reinterpret a vague sense of presence or a shadowy form as the expected ghost child. To compound the problem, many of the reports are at second- or third-hand, or an even greater remove.

Researching tales like that of the Holiday Inn's child specter can be illuminating. In that case there is no evidence to support claims made by Dennis William Hauck, author of *Haunted Places: The National Directory*, of "a little girl who was burned to death in a house that formerly stood on the site." The Grand Island historian was unable to document any deadly fire at that locale. The only known blaze at the site occurred in 1963, at which time the historic John Nice mansion had been transformed into a restaurant, and there was not a single fatality. My search of the nearby White-haven Cemetery, where the Nice family is buried, failed to turn up any credible candidate for the role of ghost-girl, least of all one named "Tanya"—which, as census and cemetery records show, was not the name of any of John Nice's ten daughters. . . .

Good for Business

Ghost tales may indeed be good for business. Explained an owner of one restaurant with bar, which, according to Arthur Myers, author of *The Ghostly Register*, "had a reputation for having ghosts": "It was good conversation for the kind of business we're in. I never tried to dissuade anyone." Other proprietors may go even further. An alleged ghost at the Kennebunk Inn in Kennebunk, Maine, may have originated with the purchase of the inn by one of its earlier owners. He reportedly told a bartender one night that he was "going to make up a story about a ghost," presumably to promote the inn. Years later the former bartender related the story to the current owner, who in turn told me. . . .

Hoaxes do occur. For example, I caught one pranking

"ghost" flagrante delecto. In 1999 I accompanied a teacher and ten high school students from Denver's Colorado Academy on an overnight stay in a "haunted" hotel. Located in the Rocky Mountains, in the old mining town of Fairplay (where an art teacher conducts "ghost tours"), the Hand Hotel was built in 1931. In the early evening as we gathered in the lobby beneath mounted elk heads and bear skins, the lights of the chandelier flickered mysteriously. But the teacher and I both spied the surreptitious action of the desk clerk, whose sheepish smile acknowledged that one brief hotel mystery had been solved.

Other signs of pranking there included a "ghost" photo (displayed in a lobby album) that the clerk confided to me was staged, and some pennies, placed on the back of a men's room toilet, that from time to time would secretly become rearranged to form messages—like the word "why?" that I encountered. This obvious running prank invited other mischief makers (like one student) to join in.

Enter "Psychics"

Ghostly presences are hyped at many inns when "psychics" visit the premises. One session at the Farnsworth House was part of a television production for Halloween, an indication of how much credibility should be afforded it. Brookdale Lodge, near Santa Cruz, California (which I investigated for a Discovery Channel documentary that aired May 24, 1998), once invited Sylvia Browne. A regular on the *Montel Williams* TV show, the self-claimed clairvoyant and medium envisioned a ghost girl that she named "Sara," helping to bring the total number of entities thus far "detected" at Brookdale to forty-nine—and counting. Such psychics typically offer unsubstantiated, even unverifiable claims, or information that is already known. This may be gleaned in advance from research sources or obtained by the "psychic" from persons who have such knowledge through the technique of "cold reading" (an artful method of fishing for information employed by shrewd fortunetellers). Alternatively, the psychic may make numerous pronouncements, trusting that others will count the apparent hits and ignore, or interpret appropriately, the misses.

This is not to say that all such pronouncements are insincere. Those who fancy themselves psychics may exhibit the traits associated with a "fantasy-prone" personality. That is a designation for an otherwise normal person with an unusual ability to fantasize. As a child, he or she may have an imaginary playmate and live much of the time in make-believe worlds. As an adult, the person continues to spend much time fantasizing, and may report apparitional, out-of-body, or near-death experiences; claim psychic or healing powers; receive special messages from higher beings; be easily hypnotized; and/or exhibit other traits. Anyone may have some of these traits, but fantasizers have them in profusion. Sylvia Browne, for example, as a child had what her parents called "made-up friends," particularly a "spirit guide"—still with her—that she named "Francine." Browne undergoes "trances" in which "Francine" provides alleged information from "Akashic records, individual spirit guides, and messages from the Godhead." Browne also claims to see apparitions, talk to ghosts, have clairvoyant visions, make psychic medical diagnoses, divine past lives, etc. She has even started her own religion, Novus Spiritus ("New Spirit").

The use of psychics is a stock in trade of many so-called parapsychologists. Among them is Hans Holzer, one of whose many books bills him as "the world's leading expert on haunted houses" while another avows that his "cases" were "carefully investigated under scientifically stringent conditions." Unfortunately, these claims are belied by Holzer's credulous acceptance of "spirit" photos, anecdotal reports, and other doubtful evidence. For example, he "investigated" a former stagecoach inn at Thousand Oaks, California, by relying on self-styled "witch" Sybil Leek (1922–1982). In one room Leek "complained of being cold all over" and "felt" that a man had been murdered there. No verification was provided and Holzer admits she "did not connect with a female ghost whose 'presence' had been 'sensed'" by the inn's owners. Nevertheless Holzer casually opines that "Like inns in general, this one may have more undiscovered ghosts hanging on the spot."

Professional psychics like Sybil Leek and Sylvia Browne aside, we may wonder whether ordinary "ghost" percipients also have similar tendencies toward fantasizing. Over nearly three decades of ghost investigating I have noticed a pattern. In interviewing residents or staff of an allegedly haunted site, I would usually find a few who had no ghostly experiences—for example a bell captain at La Fonda Inn in Santa Fe who had spent forty-three years there. Others might have moderate experiences—like hearing a strange noise or witnessing some unexplained physical occurrence such as a door mysteriously opening—that they attributed to a ghost. Often, those interviewed would direct me to one or more persons whom they indicated had had intensive haunting encounters, including seeing apparitions, in short, I usually found a spectrum that ranged from outright skepticism to mediumistic experiences. I also sensed a difference in the people: some appeared down-to-earth and level-headed, while others—I thought—seemed more imaginative and impulsive, recounting with dramatic flair their phantomesque adventures. I had no immediate way of objectively measuring what I thought I was observing, but I gave it much thought.

At length I developed a questionnaire that, on the one hand, measures the number and intensity of ghostly experiences, and, on the other, counts the number of exhibited traits associated with fantasy-proneness. Tabulation of a limited number of questionnaires administered thus far shows a strong correlation between these two areas—that, as the level of haunting experiences rises, the fantasy scale tends to show a similarly high score.

As this and other evidence indicates, to date there is no credible scientific evidence that inns—or any other sites—are inhabited by spirits of the dead. As Robert A. Baker often remarks, "There are no haunted places, only haunted people."

"*A series of carefully documented case studies raises the possibility that some intuitions are due to a genuine sixth sense.*"

Some Evidence Indicates That Psychic Ability Exists

Dean Radin

There is evidence that suggests that humans have an ability to predict the future, maintains Dean Radin in the following viewpoint. According to Radin, scientific experiments have revealed that many people have an intuitive recognition, or "gut feeling," before something bad happens. These experiments entailed measuring several individuals' skin resistance and blood flow before, during, and after they were shown a series of photographs. Researchers found that people often physiologically react to a shocking or emotional picture *before* they actually see it. These physical responses are not discernable to the perceivers, Radin points out, suggesting that this "sixth sense" generally operates at an unconscious level. Radin, a parapsychologist and researcher, is president of the Boundary Institute, a nonprofit scientific research institute in Los Altos, California.

As you read, consider the following questions:
1. According to Radin, what kinds of prosaic explanations might account for many seemingly intuitive hunches?
2. What independent experiments indicate the existence of psychic abilities, according to the author?
3. How might the discovery of a sixth sense change society, in Radin's opinion?

Alex, a university colleague, was cleaning his double-action, six-shot revolver in preparation for a hunting trip later in the month. In this pistol, when the trigger is pulled the hammer is cocked, the cylinder revolves, and the hammer falls on the next chamber, all in one smooth motion. For safety's sake, Alex normally kept five bullets in the revolver, with the hammer resting on the sixth, empty chamber.

Before cleaning the gun, he later told me, he removed the five bullets and set them aside. When finished cleaning, he began to put the bullets back in the cylinder. When he arrived at the fifth and final bullet, he suddenly got a distinct sense of dread. It had something to do with that bullet.

Alex was bothered about the odd feeling because nothing like it had ever happened to him before. He decided to trust his gut, so he put the bullet aside and positioned the pistol's hammer as usual over the sixth chamber. The chamber next to it, which normally held the fifth bullet, was now also empty.

Two weeks later, Alex was at a hunting lodge with his fiancée and her parents. That evening, unexpectedly, a violent argument broke out between the parents. Alex tried to calm them down, but the father, in an insane rage, grabbed Alex's gun, which had been in a drawer, and pointed it at his wife.

Alex tried to intervene by jumping between the gun and the woman, but he was too late—the trigger was already being pulled. For a horrifying split second, Alex knew that he was about to get shot at point-blank range. But instead of a sudden, gruesome death, the pistol went "click." The cylinder had revolved to an empty chamber—the very chamber that would have contained the fifth bullet if Alex had not set it aside two weeks earlier.

Intuitive Hunches

Had Alex actually predicted the future, or was this just an extraordinary coincidence? There are several possible explanations for why such "intuitive hunches" sometimes play out. One is that on a subconscious level, we are always thinking and coming to conclusions, but that these register only as hunches to our conscious mind. Another is that we pick up telling cues from body language, subliminal sounds or peripheral vision without being consciously aware of doing so.

A third is that for each amazing coincidence we remember, we forget all the times we had a hunch and it didn't pan out. A fourth possibility is that we modify our memories for our own convenience, creating a connection where it may not have existed. And so on. These sorts of prosaic explanations probably account for many intuitive hunches. But they don't explain them all.

As in the case of Alex's intuition, a series of carefully documented case studies raises the possibility that some intuitions are due to a genuine sixth sense. But to confirm that those stories are what they appear to be, we must turn to controlled laboratory tests.

In a pilot study and in three follow-up experiments, I have observed that many people respond unconsciously to something bad—even before it happens. Take the prototypical case of a well-known editor of a popular magazine. When she asks the question, "Is there a sixth sense?" I don't answer directly. I ask if she'd like to participate in an experiment that uses pictures randomly selected by computer, and she agrees.

An Experiment

I have her sit before a blank computer screen. All I've told her is that she's about to see a series of digitized photographs. Some will be calm, like a placid lake, and others will be emotional, like a big spider. On two fingers of her left hand, I attach electrodes that measure tiny changes in her skin resistance. On a third finger I place an electrode that monitors blood flow. I explain that all she has to do is press the button on the mouse when she's ready to begin, and then look at the pictures.

I leave the room, she relaxes, and then she presses the button. For five seconds, the screen remains blank, and then the computer randomly selects one picture out of a large pool of photos—some calming and some provocative. The picture is displayed for three seconds, and then the screen goes blank for eight seconds. Finally, a message appears announcing that she can start the next trial whenever she's ready.

She repeats this sequence 40 times. At the end of the experiment, I analyze the data recorded by the electrodes and prepare two summary graphs. Each graph shows average changes in her skin resistance and blood flow before, during and after she saw either calm or emotional pictures. What she immediately notices is that after she viewed the emotional pictures, both her skin resistance and fingertip blood flow dramatically changed. And after she viewed calm pictures, her physiology hardly changed at all.

"So I responded emotionally when I saw something emotional, and I remained calm when I saw something calm," she says. "How does that demonstrate a sixth sense?"

I direct her attention to the segment of the graph showing her responses before the computer selected the pictures. "This bump shows that your body responded to emotional pictures before the computer selected them. And this flat line," I say, pointing to the other line, "shows that your body did not respond before calm pictures were shown. You see? Your body was responding to your future emotion before the computer randomly selected an emotional or calm picture."

As this sinks in, I add, "We can now demonstrate in the laboratory what at some level we've known all along: Many people literally get a gut feeling before something bad happens. Our viscera warn us of danger even if our conscious mind doesn't always get the message."

Presentiment

Our editor's body showed signs of what I call presentiment, an unconscious form of "psi" perception. Psi is a neutral term for psychic experiences, and though it sounds like fodder for an episode of the *X-Files*, scientists around the world have studied the subject in the laboratory for over a century. The scientific evidence is now stronger than ever for commonly reported experiences such as telepathy (mind-to-mind communication), clairvoyance (information received from a distant place) and precognition (information received from a distant time). Studies suggest that we have ways of gaining information that bypass the ordinary senses. The sixth sense and similar terms, like second sight and extrasensory perception (ESP), refer to perceptual experiences that transcend the usual boundaries of space and time.

In trying to take these findings further, I realized that we have to dig deeper than what's detectable at the conscious level. While ESP and psi generally refer to conscious psychic experiences, I've always thought that asking people to consciously report subtle psi impressions was a shot in the dark. What would happen if we bypassed the psychological defense mechanisms that filter our perceptions and censor our conscious awareness? Would we find psi experiences that people weren't aware of?

Research in Parapsychology

Contemporary psi [psychic phenomena] research is usually considered to have begun in 1927, when Joseph Banks Rhine and his wife/collaborator, Louisa, arrived in the psychology department at Duke University in Durham, North Carolina. Rhine's experiments, which tested for ESP with decks of cards containing geometric symbols, became well known to the general public in 1937 when he published *New Frontiers of the Mind.* The book received widespread press coverage and became a Book of the Month Club selection. Even today, many Americans know of Rhine's work.

Since Rhine, many parapsychologists have reported positive psi results using a wide variety of experimental procedures. Yet most academic psychologists are not yet persuaded that the existence of psi has been established.

Daryl J. Bem, *World & I*, August 1994.

A handful of colleagues have paved the way for this type of investigation. In the mid-1960s, psychologist Charles Tart, Ph.D., of the University of California at Davis, measured skin conductance, blood volume, heart rate, and verbal reports between two people, called a sender-receiver pair. He, as the sender, received random electrical shocks to see if remote receivers could detect those events. Tart found that while they weren't consciously aware of anything out of the ordinary, the distant receivers' physiology registered significant reactions to the shocks he experienced.

In other, independent experiments, engineer Douglas Dean at the Newark College of Engineering; psychologist Jean Barry, Ph.D., in France; and psychologist Erlendur Haraldsson, Ph.D., at the University of Utrecht, all observed significant changes in receivers' finger blood volume when a sender, located thousands of miles away, directed emotional thoughts toward them. The journal *Science* also published a study by two physiologists who reported finding significant correlations in brain waves between isolated identical twins. These sorts of studies came to be known as Distant Mental Intention on Living Systems (DMILS).

The idea for studying intuitive hunches came to me in 1993, while I was a research fellow in the psychology department at the University of Edinburgh in Scotland. I was investigating the "feeling of being stared at." In the laboratory, I separated two people, placing them in rooms that were 100 feet away from each another. Then I monitored person #1's electrodermal activity while person #2 stared at person #1 over a one-way closed-circuit video system. Although the stared-at person could have no conscious idea when the "starer" was doing the looking, since the two were in different rooms and the staring occurred at random times, I did observe small changes in the skin resistance of the person being stared at over closed-circuit television.

In thinking about this result, I realized that (for relativistic reasons) this sort of "nonlocal" connection across space implied a complementary connection across time. If we were seeing a genuine space-separated effect between people, then the same thing ought to work as a time-separated effect within one person. I called this proposed effect "presentiment" because the term suggests a response to a future emotional event.

Additional Tests

I soon discovered that even the staunchest skeptics, those ready to swear on a stack of scientific journals that psi was impossible, were somewhat less critical of intuitive hunches. That's because most people have had at least one.

I myself hardly believed the results of the studies I conducted on the magazine editor and others. But I couldn't find any mistakes in the study design or analysis of the results. Some months later, Dick Bierman, Ph.D., a professor at the University of Amsterdam, learned of my studies and couldn't believe them either. So he repeated the experiment in his lab and found the same results. Since then, two students of psychologist Robert Morris, Ph.D., at the University of Edinburgh, have also repeated the study, and again found similar results. More replication attempts are now under way in several other laboratories.

Do our experiments prove without question that the sixth sense exists? Not yet. What we have are three independent labs reporting similar effects based on data from more than 200 participants. The proof of the pudding will rest upon many more labs getting the same results. Still, our studies, combined with the outcomes of many other types of tests by dozens of investigators on precognition and other classes of psi phenomena, have caused even highly skeptical scientists to ponder what was previously unthinkable—the possibility of a genuine sixth sense.

In 1995, for example, no less an arch-skeptic than the late astronomer Carl Sagan rendered his lifelong opinion that all psi effects were impossible. But in one of his last books, *The Demon-Haunted World: Science as a Candle in the Dark*, he wrote, "At the time of writing there are three claims in the ESP field which, in my opinion, deserve serious study: (1) that by thought alone humans can (barely) affect random number generators in computers; (2) that people under mild sensory deprivation can receive thoughts or images "projected" at them; and (3) that young children sometimes report the details of a previous life, which upon checking turn out to be accurate and which they could not have known about in any other way than reincarnation."

The Effect on Society

If scientists eventually agree that a sixth sense exists, how might this change society? On one hand, it may change nothing; we may learn that genuine psi abilities are rare and only weakly predictive, and thus inconsequential for most practical purposes.

On the other hand, it's possible that the study of the sixth sense will revolutionize our understanding of causality and have radically new applications. For example, in the January 2000 issue of *Alternative Therapies*, psychologist William Braud, Ph.D., professor and research director at the Institute of Transpersonal Psychology and co-director of the Institute's William James Center for Consciousness Studies, discusses the concept of "retroactive intentional influence" as applied to healing. He poses the idea that in cases where serious illnesses disappear virtually overnight, perhaps a healer went back in time to jumpstart the healing process.

Braud is well aware of the mind-bending nature of this hypothesis, but it is not purely fantastical. In his article, he reviews several hundred experiments examining a wide range of retrocausal phenomena, from mental influence of random numbers generated by electronic circuits, to guessing picture targets selected in the future, to studies examining the "feeling of being stared at," to presentiment experiments. He concludes that this sizable but not well-known body of carefully controlled research indicates that some form of retroactive intentional influence is indeed possible, and may have important consequences for healing.

A less radical application might be for early warning systems. Imagine that on a future aircraft all the members of the flight crew are connected to an onboard computer system. The system is designed to continuously monitor heart rate, electrical activity in the skin, and blood flow. Before the crew comes aboard, each person is calibrated to see how he or she responds before, during and after different kinds of emotional and calm events. Each person's idiosyncratic responses are used to create a person-unique emotional "response template," which is fed into the computer.

While the plane is in the air, the computer monitors each crew member's body to assess their emotional level. If the computer detects that all crew members are about to have an emotional response (and the aircraft is otherwise operating normally), then the computer could alert the pilot. Sometimes even a few seconds of advance warning in an aircraft can save the lives of everyone on board.

Very likely, some intuitive hunches do indicate the presence of a sixth sense. But for whom? Probably everyone, to a degree. But just as some people have poor vision, it is also quite likely that some people are effectively "psi-blind." I suspect that in the future, with a little assistance from specialized technologies, the same way a hearing aid can improve poor hearing, it may become possible to boost our weak sixth sense.

> *"Statistics can reveal the truth when pseudoscience is being flogged to an unsuspecting group."*

The Existence of Psychic Ability Has Not Been Proven

Michael Shermer

In the following viewpoint, Michael Shermer contends that the existence of human psychic ability such as ESP has not been proven. To support his point, Shermer describes his tour of the Association for Research and Enlightenment, an organization founded to investigate ESP and other psychic powers. During his visit, Shermer volunteered to participate in a group experiment that was supposed to reveal if one had ESP. Although the testers claimed that several individuals scored "high marks" indicating that they had psychic ability, Shermer saw that the results showed nothing more than the effect of random chance. Those who peddle pseudoscience often misinterpret statistics to achieve their desired results, the author concludes. Shermer is the author of *Why People Believe Weird Things: Pseudoscience, Superstition, and Other Confusions of Our Time*, from which this viewpoint is excerpted.

As you read, consider the following questions:

1. According to Shermer, what are some of the classes offered by the Association of Research and Enlightenment (A.R.E.)?
2. Who was Edgar Cayce, according to the author?
3. According to Shermer, how did one of the A.R.E. tour guides react when asked if his ESP abilities had improved over the years?

O ne of the most overused one-liners in the statistical business is Disraeli's classification (and Mark Twain's clarifi-
cation) of lies into the three taxa "lies, damn lies, and statistics." Of course, the problem really lies in the misuse of
statistics and, more generally, in the misunderstanding of
statistics and probabilities that most of us have in dealing with
the real world. When it comes to estimating the likelihood of
something happening, most of us overestimate or underesti-
mate probabilities in a way that can make normal events seem
like paranormal phenomena. I saw a classic example of this in
a visit to Edgar Cayce's Association for Research and Enlightenment (A.R.E.), located in Virginia Beach, Virginia.
One day when I was in town, Clay Drees, a professor at
nearby Virginia Wesleyan College, and I decided to pay them
a visit. We were fortunate to arrive on a relatively busy day
during which the A.R.E. staff were conducting an ESP "experiment" in extrasensory perception (ESP). Since they were
claiming that one's ESP could be proved scientifically, we
considered A.R.E. fair game for skeptics.

The Association for Research and Enlightenment

According to their own literature, A.R.E. was "founded in
1931 to preserve, research, and make available the readings
of Edgar Cayce," one of the most prominent "psychics" of
the twentieth century. Like many such organizations, A.R.E.
has many of the trappings of science: a building whose size
and façade suggest modernity and authority; an extensive research library containing both the psychic readings of Edgar
Cayce and a fairly good science and pseudoscience collection
(though they do not classify their holdings this way); a bookstore selling a full array of writings on the paranormal, including books on spiritual living, self-discovery, inner help,
past lives, health, longevity, healing, native wisdom, and the
future. A.R.E. describes itself as "a research organization"
that "continues to index and catalogue information, to initi-
ate investigation and experiments, and to promote conferences, seminars, and lectures."

The corpus of accepted beliefs reads like an A-to-Z who's
who and what's what of the paranormal. The circulating files
index of the library includes the following psychic readings

from Cayce: angels and archangels, astrological influences on Earth experiences, economic healing, evaluating psychic talent, intuition, visions and dreams, Karma and the law of grace, magnetic healing, the missing years of Jesus, the oneness of life and death, planetary sojourns and astrology, principles of psychic science, reincarnation, soul retrogression, and vibrations, to name just a few. A "reading" consisted of Cayce reclining in a chair, closing his eyes, going into an "altered state," and dictating hours of material. During his lifetime, Cayce dictated no less than fourteen thousand psychic readings on over ten thousand subjects! A separate medical library has its own circulating files index listing Cayce's psychic readings on every imaginable disease and its cure. One is "Edgar Cayce's famous 'Black Book,'" which will give you a "simple scar removal formula," explain "the best hours of sleep," tell you "the best exercise," clarify what "will help the memory," and, on page 209, solve that most mysterious of medical conundrums, "how to get rid of bad breath."

A.R.E. also has its own press—the A.R.E. Publishing Company—and incorporates the Atlantic University of Transpersonal Studies. The latter offers an "independent studies program" that includes the following courses: "TS 501—Introduction to Transpersonal Studies" (the works of Cayce, Abraham Maslow, Victor Frankl, and Buddhism); "TS 503—The Origin and Development of Human Consciousness" (on ancient magicians and the great mother goddess), "TS 504—Spiritual Philosophies and the Nature of Humanity" (on spiritual creation and evolution), "TS 506—The Inner Life: Dream, Meditation, and Imaging" (dreams as problem-solving tools), "TS 508—Religious Traditions" (Hinduism, Buddhism, Judaism, Islam, and Christianity), and "TS 518—Divination as a Way to Measure All" (astrology, tarot, I Ching, handwriting analysis, palmistry, and psychic readings).

A potpourri of lectures and seminars encourages followers' beliefs and provides opportunities for the uninitiated to get involved. A lecture on "Egypt, Myth, and Legend," by Ahmed Fayed, articulates a not-so-hidden agenda: Cayce's life in ancient Egypt. "Naming the Name: Choosing Jesus the Christ as Your Living Master" demonstrates A.R.E.'s openness to more traditional religions and its lack of discrimination between any and all belief systems. A "Sounding and Overtone Chanting" seminar promises to equip you with "tools for empowerment and transformation." A three-day seminar called "The Healing Power of Past-Life Memories" features, among others, Raymond Moody, who claims that the near-death experience is a bridge to the other side.

Edgar Cayce

Who was Edgar Cayce? According to A.R.E. literature, Cayce was born in 1877 on a farm near Hopkinsville, Kentucky. As a youth, he "displayed powers of perception which extended beyond the five senses. Eventually, he would become the most documented psychic of all times." Purportedly, when he was twenty-one, Cayce's doctors were unable to find a cause or cure for a "gradual paralysis which threatened the loss of his voice." Cayce responded by going into a "hypnotic sleep" and recommended a cure for himself, which he claims worked. The discovery of his ability to diagnose illnesses and recommend solutions while in an altered state led him to do this on a regular basis for others with medical problems. This, in turn, expanded into general psychic readings on thousands of different topics covering every conceivable aspect of the universe, the world, and humanity.

Numerous books have been written on Edgar Cayce, some by uncritical followers and others by skeptics. Skeptic Martin Gardner demonstrates that Cayce was fantasy-prone from his youth, often talking with angels and receiving visions of his dead grandfather. Uneducated beyond the ninth grade, Cayce acquired his broad knowledge through voracious reading, and from this he wove elaborate tales and gave detailed diagnoses while in his trances. His early psychic readings were done in the presence of an osteopath, from whom he borrowed much of his terminology. When his wife got tuberculosis, Cayce offered this diagnosis: "The condition in the body is quite different from what we have had before . . . from the head, pains along through the body from the second, fifth and sixth dorsals, and from the first and second lumbar . . . tie-ups here, and floating lesions, or lateral lesions, in the muscular and nerve fibers." As Gardner explains, "This is talk which makes sense to an osteopath, and to almost no one else."

In Cayce, skeptic James Randi sees all the familiar tricks of the psychic trade: "Cayce was fond of expressions like 'I feel that . . .' and 'perhaps'—qualifying words used to avoid positive declarations." Cayce's remedies read like prescriptions from a medieval herbalist: for a leg sore, use oil of smoke; for a baby with convulsions, a peach-tree poultice; for dropsy, bedbug juice; for arthritis, peanut oil massage; and for his wife's tuberculosis, ash from the wood of a bamboo tree. Were Cayce's readings and diagnoses correct? Did his remedies work? It is hard to say. Testimony from a few patients does not represent a controlled experiment, and among his more obvious failures are several patients who died between the time of writing to Cayce and Cayce's reading. In one such instance, according to Randi, Cayce did a reading on a small girl in which he recommended a complex nutritional program to cure the disease but admonished, "And this depends upon whether one of the things as intended to be done today is done or isn't done, see?" The girl had died the day before, however.

An ESP Experiment

It was, then, with considerable anticipation that we passed under the words "That we may make manifest the love of God and man" and entered into the halls of Edgar Cayce's legacy. Inside there were no laboratory rooms and no scientific equipment save an ESP machine proudly displayed against a wall in the entrance hall. A large sign next to the machine announced that shortly there would be an ESP experiment in an adjacent room. We saw our opportunity.

The ESP machine featured the standard Zener cards (created by K.E. Zener, they display easily distinguished shapes to be interpreted in Psi experiments), with a button to push for each of the five symbols—plus sign, square, star, circle, and wavy lines. One of the directors of A.R.E. began with a lecture on ESP, Edgar Cayce, and the development of psychic powers. He explained that some people are born with a psychic gift while others need practice, but we all have the power to some degree. When he asked for participants, I volunteered to be a receiver. I was given no instruction on how to receive psychic messages, so I asked. The instructor explained that I should concentrate on the sender's forehead. The thirty-four other people in the room were told to do the same thing. We were all given an ESP Testing Score Sheet, with paired columns for our psychic choices and the correct answers, given after the experiment. We ran two trials of 25 cards each. I got 7 right in the first set, for which I honestly tried to receive the message, and 3 right in the second set, for which I marked the plus sign for every card.

The Tricky Brain

People can be tricked by their own brain. This view is based on my conviction that the human brain is basically a kind of computer. What happens in a computer when new data are stored? These data receive a time stamp. A clever programmer can simply change that time stamp. Compared with events that are registered later, those antedated data might appear to be a "paranormal signal." In other words, the "memory" of a computer can be sabotaged. The same kind of thing can happen to people. One can have a shocking experience, and then remember with "absolute certainty" that one has dreamt the incident the week before. How can one be sure? How can one know that the brain hasn't antedated the memory? Sometimes the brain can have an interest in making such errors. . . . Our memory is far from infallible, and I think that an important class of paranormal "events" are the result of the brain antedating memories or maybe even fabricating memories that have no relation to reality. The individual to which this happens has no way of separating the true from the false memories.

Gerard t'Hooft, *Skeptical Inquirer*, March 2000.

The instructor explained that "5 right is average, chance is between 3 and 7, and anything above 7 is evidence of ESP." I asked, "If 3 to 7 is chance, and anything above 7 is evidence of ESP, what about someone who scores below a 3?" The instructor responded, "That's a sign of negative ESP." (He didn't say what that was.) I then surveyed the group. In the first set, three people got 2 right, while another three got 8 right; in the second set, one even got 9 right. So, while I apparently did not have psychic power, at least four other people did. Or did they?

Random Results

Before concluding that high scores indicate a high degree of ESP ability, you have to know what kind of scores people would get purely by chance. The scores expected by chance can be predicted by probability theory and statistical analysis. Scientists use comparisons between statistically predicted test results and actual test results to determine whether results are significant, that is, better than what would be expected by chance. The ESP test results clearly matched the expected pattern for random results.

I explained to the group, "In the first set, three got 2, three got 8, and everyone else [twenty-nine people] scored between 3 and 7. In the second set, there was one 9, two 2s, and one 1, *all scored by different people than those who scored high and low in the first test!* Doesn't that sound like a normal distribution around an average of 5?" The instructor turned and said, with a smile, "Are you an engineer or one of those statisticians or something?" The group laughed, and he went back to lecturing about how to improve your ESP with practice.

When he asked for questions, I waited until no one else had any and then inquired, "You say you've been working with A.R.E. for several decades, correct?" He nodded. "And you say that with experience one can improve ESP, right?" He immediately saw where I was going and said, "Well . . . ," at which point I jumped in and drew the conclusion, "By now you must be very good at this sort of test. How about we send the signals to you at the machine. I'll bet you could get at least 15 out of the 25." He was not amused at my suggestion and explained to the group that he had not practiced ESP in a long time and, besides, we were out of time for the experiment. He quickly dismissed the group, upon which a handful of people surrounded me and asked for an explanation of what I meant by "a normal distribution around an average of 5."

On a piece of scrap paper, I drew a crude version of the normal frequency curve, more commonly known as the bell curve. I explained that the mean, or average number, of correct responses ("hits") is expected by chance to be 5 (5 out of 25). The amount that the number of hits will deviate from the standard mean of 5, by chance, is 2. Thus, for a group this size, we should not put any special significance on the fact that someone got 8 correct or someone scored only 1 or 2 correct hits. This is exactly what is expected to happen by chance.

So these test results suggest that nothing other than chance was operating. The deviation from the mean for this experiment was nothing more than what we would expect. If the audience were expanded into the millions, say on a television show, there would be an even bigger opportunity for misinterpretation of the high scores. In this scenario, a tiny fraction would be 3 standard deviations above the mean, or get 11 hits, a still smaller percentage would reach 4 standard deviations, or 13 hits, and so on, all as predicted by chance and the randomness of large numbers. Believers in psychic power tend to focus on the results of the most deviant subjects (in the statistical sense) and tout them as the proof of the power. But statistics tells us that given a large enough group, there should be someone who will score fairly high. There may be lies and damned lies, but statistics can reveal the truth when pseudoscience is being flogged to an unsuspecting group.

Unsinkable Rubber Ducks

After the ESP experiment, one woman followed me out of the room and said, "You're one of those skeptics, aren't you?"

"I am indeed," I responded.

"Well, then," she retorted, "how do you explain coincidences like when I go to the phone to call my friend and she calls me? Isn't that an example of psychic communication?"

"No, it is not," I told her. "It is an example of statistical coincidences. Let me ask you this: How many times did you go to the phone to call your friend and she did not call? Or how many times did your friend call you but you did not call her first?"

She said she would have to think about it and get back to me. Later, she found me and said she had figured it out: "I only remember the times that these events happen, and I forget all those others you suggested."

"Bingo!" I exclaimed, thinking I had a convert. "You got it. It is just selective perception."

But I was too optimistic. "No," she concluded, "this just proves that psychic power works sometimes but not others."

As James Randi says, believers in the paranormal are like "unsinkable rubber ducks."

"The [witnesses] should be more than enough to convince anyone with an open mind that something quite extraordinary occurred at Roswell in the summer of 1947."

The Government Is Covering Up Evidence of a UFO Crash

Jim Marrs

In July 1947, an unusual object crashed on a ranch near Roswell, New Mexico. According to Jim Marrs, the author of the following viewpoint, this object was most likely an extraterrestrial spacecraft. Several eyewitnesses reported seeing strange debris and small humanoid bodies with large heads and eyes, writes Marrs. Although government officials now claim that the wreckage was that of a secret military balloon, the government's past record of lies and deceit casts doubt on this explanation. Marrs, a journalist based in Dallas, Texas, is the author of *Alien Agenda*, from which this viewpoint is excerpted.

As you read, consider the following questions:

1. When and why did investigators begin challenging the official explanation for the Roswell crash, according to Marrs?
2. According to witnesses Bill Brazel and Sallye Tadolini, what was unusual about the debris that was recovered at the crash site?
3. What did New Mexico representative Steven Schiff discover when he conducted a document search on records of the Roswell incident, according to the author?

No UFO story has captured the imagination of the public as has the reported crash at Roswell, New Mexico. It remains one of the most well documented of UFO issues, yet there is no clear consensus even now on what actually happened.

To search for the truth, one should first consider a chronological account of the matter.

The story began on Tuesday, July 1, 1947, when radar installations in New Mexico started tracking an object that zigzagged across the state, exhibiting unconventional speeds and maneuvering ability. On Wednesday, an object was sighted over Roswell. On Thursday, some Washington officials flew in to observe the object.

Late Friday night, the object was lost on radar screens and believed crashed.

Wreckage on a Ranch

Saturday, July 5, Grady L. "Barney" Barnett claimed he, along with some archeologists who happened to be working north of Roswell, discovered wreckage and reported it. The Roswell Volunteer Fire Department was called to the scene, which was on a ranch thirty-five miles north of Roswell. The rancher, William "Mac" Brazel, found debris scattered over an area three-quarters of a mile long and several hundred feet wide—so much debris that his sheep refused to walk through it. On Sunday, July 6, Brazel drove to town and talked to the sheriff, who suggested that the military be notified. Soon, military units arrived and cordoned off the area. Later in the day, Brazel spoke with air intelligence officer Maj. Jesse A. Marcel and showed him a piece of the debris. Brazel returned to his base and notified higher authorities that something unusual had occurred. By Monday, July 7, a systematic examination of Brazel's field by the military began, including an air search.

Early on Tuesday morning Major Marcel stopped by his home as he returned to the airfield and showed unusual material to his wife and son. The military authorities must have felt the debris did not constitute a serious security problem, for later that morning the information officer of the 509th Bomb Group at Roswell Army Air Field—the only unit armed with atomic weapons at the time—was authorized to issue a press release announcing that the military had recovered a "flying disc." This stirred media interest all over the world. That afternoon, Major Marcel was ordered to fly with the debris to Carswell Air Force Base in Fort Worth, Texas.

Meanwhile in Washington, higher military authorities either learned of new developments—some researchers believe they had learned of the discovery of the main body of the UFO and alien bodies by military searchers—or had second thoughts about publicizing the debris. According to the Associated Press, Deputy Chief of the Army Air Forces Lt. Gen. Hoyt S. Vandenberg moved to take control of the news out of Roswell. On Tuesday evening, 8th Air Force commander Brig. Gen. Roger Ramey from his Carswell office told newsmen that Marcel and others had been mistaken and that the "flying disc" actually was nothing more than a weather balloon. Ramey's weather officer, Warrant Officer Irving Newton, was brought in and identified the debris he saw as belonging to a weather balloon. Photographers were allowed to take pictures of the "balloon" wreckage. Years later, researchers Kevin D. Randle and Donald R. Schmitt claimed the original debris was replaced by balloon wreckage in Ramey's office minutes before newsmen were ushered inside.

Following announcement of the balloon explanation, media interest quickly faded. In those security-conscious days following World War II, with fear of Russian attack becoming a way of life, no one thought to question the official version. There the matter rested until 1978, when Jesse Marcel broke his silence, telling UFO researchers Stanton Friedman and Leonard Stringfield that the object he recovered was not from the earth. Since then, the story of the Roswell crash has become a focal point of UFO research, spawning dozens of books, TV documentaries, and videos.

Conflicting Mind-Sets

There can be no doubt that something dropped out of the skies near Roswell on July 4, 1947. The question is what. We encounter conflicting mind-sets. One mind-set accepts the official explanation that a secret military balloon crashed, somehow was mistaken for a spaceship by otherwise competent intelligence officers, and was hidden away for security's sake for almost a half-century. Another accepts that a downed spacecraft containing alien bodies was recovered by the military and hidden from the public.

Everyone agrees that no spaceship wreckage or alien bodies have been made public. Therefore, the truth seeker is left with only human testimony and official pronouncements. The basis for accepting the balloon version rests exclusively on government reports, which deny any unusual aspect to the Roswell case. A lengthy recitation of past official lies, disinformation, and deceit should not be necessary to establish that such pronouncements cannot be accepted at face value.

Deore. © 1997 by *The Dallas Morning News*. Reprinted by permission of the Universal Press Syndicate.

Some recent theories contend that the wreckage actually was a secret test of a ten-balloon cluster device under Project Mogul, which was launched July 3 from Alamagordo, New Mexico, or a secret navy "Skyhook" balloon. If it were either of these devices, competent intelligent officers should have been able to distinguish it from a flying saucer. Furthermore, if this theory is correct, a common weather balloon must have been substituted for the Mogul or Skyhook balloon for the news photographers in Fort Worth, substantiating claims that the air force deliberately deceived the news media and the public. And if they lied about one thing, it stands to reason they would lie about another.

According to several reports, both the debris and alien bodies were taken to Roswell's military hospital, then flown first to Andrews Air Force Base in Washington and on to Wright Field at Dayton, Ohio.

Debunker Curtis Peebles scarcely mentioned alien bodies in his book, concentrating instead on the debris as exhibited in Fort Worth. Peebles gave the accounts of only four witnesses, one of whom was Barney Barnett, whose story he correctly discounts, as Barnett's location of the crash site differed from most versions and since investigators in 1990 found that Barnett's 1947 diary contained no mention of the Roswell crash. Peebles was able to state that Barnett's story was "unsupported by any documentation or additional witnesses." After alluding to some of the more outrageous theories concerning the Roswell incident, Peebles smugly concluded, "If all these extraneous stories are removed, one is left only with a few fragments in a field."

Additional Witnesses

On the other hand, consider these "additional witnesses" drawn from the well-documented book *The Truth About the UFO Crash at Roswell* by researchers Randle and Schmitt:

William Woody, watching the skies south of Roswell on July 4 with his father, saw a brilliantly glowing object with red streaks. Unlike other meteors he had seen, it was brighter, the wrong color, and took a long time to fall.

Mother Superior Mary Bernadette, from the roof of Roswell's St. Mary's Hospital, saw a bright light go to earth north of town and recorded the time as between 11:00 and 11:30 P.M. July 4, in a logbook.

Sister Capistrano, a Franciscan nun standing beside Mother Superior Bernadette at St. Mary's Hospital, also saw the object come down. . . .

James Ragsdale, a camper who saw a fiery object crash near his camp on the night of July 4. The next day, Ragsdale discovered a crashed circular craft and small bodies. He fled when the military arrived, thinking he might get in trouble. . . .

C. Curry Holden, one of several field archeologists who stumbled upon the crash site, described a "fat fuselage" without wings. He also said he saw three bodies, two outside the craft, one partially visible inside. . . .

Maj. Jesse Marcel, the Roswell intelligence officer who was first on the scene and announced the crash of a "flying disc," took pieces of strange metal that would straighten out after bending home to show his family. Although Marcel did not contradict the balloon explanation at the time, in later years he said he was correct the first time about a craft from space and that he was muzzled by military authorities. "It was not anything from this Earth. That, I'm quite sure of," Marcel said. "Being in intelligence, I was familiar with all materials used in aircraft and in air travel. This was nothing like this. It could not have been."

Dr. Jesse Marcel Jr., Major Marcel's son and an Air National Guard flight surgeon, who clearly remembered markings on the metal brought home by his father as consisting of "different geometric shapes, leaves and circles" akin to hieroglyphics. His father told him the metal came from a flying saucer, then had to explain what a flying saucer was to young Marcel. . . .

Steve MacKenzie, stationed at Roswell, tracked the object on radar for almost twenty-four hours and then visited the crash site, where he said a major from Washington took charge of the dead bodies, described as small with large heads and eyes. MacKenzie said if the object he tracked had been a weather balloon, secret or not, his superiors would have ordered him to ignore it. . . .

William W. "Mac" Brazel, owner of the crash site, said he heard an explosion during a thunderstorm on the night of July 4 and the next day, along with William Proctor, found a field full of scattered debris and described many big pieces of dull gray metal that was unusually lightweight and could not be cut or burned. Four days later, after being held by military authorities and accompanied by military officers, Brazel told the Associated Press the debris was actually found on June 14 and consisted of string, paper, some tape, and bits of metal that covered no more than two hundred yards in diameter. Oddly enough, he ended this obvious description of some sort of kite or balloon by saying, "I am sure what I found was not any weather observation balloon."

Bill Brazel, Mac's son, said his father was held for eight days by the military and released only after swearing not to discuss the incident. He told his son he was better off not knowing about it but swore what he saw was not a balloon. Bill Brazel said his father was muzzled by military authorities. He also said he handled some of the debris found later on his father's ranch and that it resembled aluminum foil but when wadded into a ball, it would straighten itself out smooth. He too said it could not be cut or burned. The younger Brazel said he showed pieces of the metal to friends.

Sallye Tadolini, the daughter of another of Mac Brazel's neighbors, told researchers that she recalled Bill Brazel showing her a piece of dull-colored metal that he balled up into his fist and, when he opened his hand, returned to its original shape. . . .

Glenn Dennis, then a mortician working for Ballard's Funeral Home in Roswell, said about 1:30 P.M. July 5, he received a call from the Roswell base mortuary officer asking if the funeral home could provide a number of small caskets that could be hermetically sealed. Dennis said he realized something strange had occurred when the officer called back and asked how to prepare a body that had been burned or left out in the elements for a time. Later that day, Dennis drove to Roswell Field to deliver an injured airman. At the base hospital he saw strange pieces of wreckage in the rear of an ambulance but soon was chased off by an officer, who told him not to talk or "somebody will be picking your bones out of the sand." A few days later, Dennis said a nurse friend told him she was called in to assist in the autopsy of three "foreign bodies" that gave off an overpowering odor. She said the bodies were small with large heads and hands with four fingers ending in pads that looked like suction cups. . . .

Brig. Gen. Arthur E. Exon was a World War II combat pilot who spent time in a German POW camp and later was stationed with the Air Material Command at Wright-Patterson Air Force Base, as it was known after Wright Field and Patterson Field merged. In recent years, Exon became the highest ranking officer to confirm that a quantity of material from Roswell arrived at Wright Field for testing by a "special project" team of lab workers. He said the material was "unusual," looked like foil, but couldn't be dented even by hammers. He also said that he flew over the crash site and was able to see where the craft had come down. Exon added that bodies were found with the main portion of the craft, which ended up in a separate location from the debris.

An Extraordinary Event

Naturally, considering the clash of mind-sets, questions have been raised about both the competency and veracity of the Roswell witnesses. But even if half of the witnesses are discounted, the remainder should be more than enough to convince anyone with an open mind that something quite extraordinary occurred at Roswell in the summer of 1947. That the incident stayed on the minds of men in power is illustrated by a story related by William Pitts. A former military man who today is a lecturer for the Society of Manufacturing Engineers, Pitts is the head of Project Blue Book, a private organization sanctioned by the U.S. Air Force to investigate UFO sightings. He said that in early 1977 he and others, including J. Allen Hynek, were summoned to a meeting regarding UFOs by Dr. Frank Press, science adviser to newly elected President Jimmy Carter. "The first question," recalled Pitts, "was regarding Roswell. What did we know about Roswell? I turned it around and ask them what they knew about Roswell and they did not reply. They went on to something else." It was not until more than a year later that UFO researchers began to hear the saucer crash story from Jesse Marcel and interest in the Roswell case was revived.

Various theories have been advanced to explain what was recovered at Roswell. These include a Rawin Target weather balloon, a Japanese Fugo balloon bomb, or a V-2 nose cone containing monkeys. None of these theories can explain away all the evidence now available about this event, and if any of these theories are correct, it would still mean the air force deceived the public when the weather balloon story was announced.

Responding to a request by New Mexico Republican representative Steven Schiff, the U.S. General Accounting Office (GAO) conducted a document search on records pertaining to the Roswell incident, which only added to the mystery. In July 1995 the GAO reported, "RAAF (Roswell Army Air Field) administrative records (from March, 1945, through December, 1949) and RAAF outgoing messages (from October, 1946, through December, 1949) were destroyed." Schiff's press liaison, Barry Bitzer, stated, "Having spent 24 years in the military, [Schiff] did express some surprise that those records were destroyed, supposedly against regulations and without traceable authorization." Only two records were found, a unit history report stating that a "flying disc" turned out to be a radar tracking balloon and an FBI teletype stating that the military reported that a high-altitude weather balloon was recovered near Roswell. Of course, it was these two reports—official pronouncements produced only after the official version was conceived—which were used by debunkers to dismiss the Roswell crash story. The FBI teletype was especially odd, as it indicated the Bureau may have been monitoring Roswell base telephones and it clearly stated a "disc" was sent to Wright Field. The teletype read, "[name blanked out] further advised that the object found resembles a high-altitude weather balloon with a radar reflector, but that telephonic conversations between their office and Wright Field had not borne out this belief. Disc and balloon being transported to Wright Field by special plane for examination."

Adding to the confusion were claims that other disc-shaped craft may have been recovered at other times and in other locations. Saucers reportedly were recovered in Paradise Valley north of Phoenix, Arizona, in October 1947; near Aztec, New Mexico, in March 1948; and in Mexico near Laredo, Texas, later in 1948. Any one of the crash stories could have been real with the others acting as red herrings, or all the stories could be false. Information on these crashes is meager compared to Roswell and involved the familiar charges and countercharges of lies and hoaxes.

The Autopsy Film

Even a purported autopsy film of an alien body recovered in 1947 has been offered as proof of the crash recovery. During 1995, Ray Santilli, owner of a small London video distribution company, caused a worldwide clamor by revealing what he claimed was authentic 1947 black-and-white movie film of the autopsy of an alien creature found in New Mexico. At first glance, the film—an "Alien Autopsy" complete with 1940s telephone, clock, and medical instruments and a "real" handheld shaky quality—seemed to offer objective evidence that alien bodies had indeed been recovered in New Mexico. . . .

Arguments raged back and forth about the legitimacy of the autopsy film until even many ufologists grew tired of the issue and it faded into the background—although no one was ever able to prove beyond question that it was a fake. Such is the fate of issues mired in the uncompromising battle between mind-sets.

Without resorting to convoluted speculation with little or no supporting evidence, it would appear that the most straightforward explanation of the Roswell story is that a very unusual craft crashed and the occupants—whether dead or alive—were taken into custody by the U.S. military, which then conducted a cover-up.

"There really had been a cover-up [of a crash near Roswell] . . . but not of an alien spaceship."

The Government Is Not Covering Up Evidence of a UFO Crash

Robert L. Park

In the following viewpoint, Robert L. Park argues that an extraterrestrial spacecraft did not crash near Roswell, New Mexico, in the summer of 1947. Recent research has shown that the wreckage that was recovered on a southwestern ranch was from a secret military project (Project Mogul) in which a large military balloon was launched to detect Soviet atomic bomb tests. The government, however, initially claimed that the wreckage was a weather balloon in an attempt to protect the secrecy of Project Mogul. But rather than dispel the Roswell UFO myth, Park writes, the discovery that the government did engage in some kind of deception has convinced conspiracy theorists that Project Mogul itself is just another cover-up. Park is a physicist at the University of Maryland in College Park and the director of the American Physical Society in Washington, D.C.

As you read, consider the following questions:
1. What was the truth about the "flying saucer" that the author encountered while driving on a highway in New Mexico?
2. What other secret government program helped to bolster belief in UFOs, according to Park?

In the summer of 1954, when I was a young Air Force lieutenant, I was sent on temporary assignment to Walker Air Force Base in Roswell, New Mexico, to oversee the installation of a new radar system. Late one night I was returning to the base after a weekend visit with my family in Texas. I was driving on a totally deserted stretch of highway. The sky was moonless but very clear, and I could make out a range of ragged hills off to my left, silhouetted against the background of stars. Suddenly the entire countryside was lit up by a dazzling blue-green light, streaking across the sky just above the horizon.

The light flashed on and off as it passed behind the hills, then vanished without a sound. It was all over in perhaps two seconds. At the time, reported sightings of unidentified flying objects—UFOs—made the news almost daily. Indeed, the town where I was stationed, Roswell, was the hub of many such speculations. But I prided myself on being a skeptical thinker, and I had little patience for wacky ideas about flying saucers invading the earth.

In fact, I had a perfectly plausible explanation for the spectacular event I had just witnessed. Pale blue-green is the characteristic color of the light emitted by certain frozen free radicals as they warm up. A free radical is a fragment of a molecule, and one well-known variety of free radical is the so-called hydroxide radical—a water molecule that is missing one of its hydrogen atoms. Free radicals are energetically predisposed to reconnect with their missing parts, and for that reason they are highly reactive: ordinarily they do not stick around very long.

But if molecules are broken up into free radicals by radiation at low temperature, the radicals can be frozen in place. Then, when the severed parts of the molecule are warmed up, they readily recombine to form the same kinds of stable molecules from which they originated. The energy that is liberated when hydroxide radicals recombine with hydrogen atoms to form water appears as blue-green fluorescence. It occurred to me that an ice meteoroid would gradually accumulate hydroxide radicals as a result of cosmic-ray bombardment. What I had had the good fortune to see just then, I reasoned, was a meteor plunging into the earth's upper atmosphere, where it warmed, setting off the recombination reaction.

A "Close Encounter"

As I continued driving down the empty highway and crossed into New Mexico, I felt rather smug. The UFO hysteria that was sweeping the country, I told myself, was for people who don't understand science. Then I saw the flying saucer.

It was off to my left, between the highway and the distant hills, racing along just above the rangeland. It appeared to be a shiny metal disk, thicker in the center than at the edges, and it was traveling at almost the same speed I was. Was it following me? I stepped hard on the gas pedal of the Oldsmobile—and the saucer accelerated. I slammed on the brakes—and it stopped. Only then could I see that it was my own headlights, reflecting off a telephone line strung parallel to the highway. The apparition no longer looked like a flying saucer at all.

It was a humbling experience. My cerebral cortex might have sneered at stories of flying saucers, but the part of my brain where those stories were stored had been activated by the powerful experience of the icy meteorite. At an unconscious level, my mind was busy making connections and associations. I was primed to see a flying saucer—and my brain filled in the details.

Who has not "seen" an animal in dusky twilight that turns into a bush as one takes a closer look? But something more than the mind playing tricks with patterns of light is needed to explain why hundreds—by some accounts thousands—of people claim to have been abducted by aliens, whisked aboard a spaceship and subjected to some kind of physical examination, usually focusing on their erogenous zones. After the examination, the aliens are frequently said to insert a miniature implant into the abductee's body. Often the memory of an abduction has a dreamlike quality, and subjects can recall the details only under hypnosis. . . .

It is hardly surprising that there are similarities in the accounts of people who claim to have been abducted by aliens. All of us have been exposed to the same images and stories in the popular media. My local bookstore stocks three times as many books about UFOs as it carries about science. Aliens stare at us from the covers of magazines and make cameo appearances in television commercials. As time goes by, the depictions become increasingly uniform. Any six-year-old can now sketch what an alien looks like. Popular culture is, in fact, undergoing a kind of alien evolution: each new creation by a filmmaker or sci-fi writer acts as a mutation, and the selection mechanism is audience approval. Aliens subtly evolve to satisfy public expectations. . . .

The "Crashed Disc" Story

The current fascination with aliens can be traced back to the strange events that took place near Roswell, New Mexico, in the summer of 1947. On June 14 of that year, William Brazel, the foreman of the Foster Ranch, seventy-five miles northwest of Roswell, spotted a large area of wreckage about seven miles from the ranch house. The debris included neoprene strips, tape, metal foil, cardboard and sticks. Brazel didn't bother to examine it closely at the time, but a few weeks later he heard about reports of flying saucers and wondered if what he had seen might be related. He went back with his wife and gathered up some of the pieces. The next day he drove to the little town of Corona, New Mexico, to sell wool, and while he was there he "whispered kind a confidential like" to the Lincoln County sheriff, George Wilcox, that he might have found pieces of one of those "flying discs" people were talking about. The sheriff reported the matter to the nearby army air base—the same base, in fact, where I would be stationed seven years later (before my time, though the Air Corps was still part of the army, and the base was known as Roswell Army Air Field).

The army sent an intelligence officer, Major Jesse Marcel, to check out the report. Marcel thought the debris looked like pieces of a weather balloon or a radar reflector; in any event, all of it fit easily into the trunk of his car. There the incident might have ended—except for the garbled account the public-information office at the base issued to the press the next day. The army, the press office noted, had "gained possession of a flying disc through the cooperation of a local rancher and the sheriff's office." The army quickly issued a correction describing the debris as a standard radar target, but it was too late. The Roswell incident had been launched. With the passage of years, the retraction of that original press release would come to look more and more like a cover-up.

Macnelly. © 1997 by *Chicago Tribune*. Reprinted with permission.

By 1978, thirty years after Brazel spotted wreckage on his ranch, actual alien bodies had begun to show up in accounts of the "crash." Major Marcel's story about loading sticks, cardboard and metal foil into the trunk of his car had mutated into the saga of a major military operation, which allegedly recovered an entire alien spaceship and secretly transported it to Wright Patterson Air Force Base in Ohio. Even as the number of people who might recall the original events dwindled, incredible new details were added by second- and third-hand sources: There was not one crash but two or three. The aliens were small, with large heads and suction cups on their fingers. One alien survived for a time but was kept hidden by the government—and on and on.

A Full-Scale Myth

Like a giant vacuum cleaner, the story had sucked in and mingled together snippets from reports of unrelated plane crashes and high-altitude parachute experiments involving anthropo-morphic dummies, even though some of those events took place years later and miles away. And, with years' worth of imaginative energy to drive their basic beliefs, various UFO "investigators" managed to stitch those snippets into a full-scale myth of an encounter with extraterrestrials—an en-counter that had been covered up by the government. The truth, according to the believers, was simply too frightening to share with the public.

Roswell became a gold mine. The unverified accounts spawned a string of profitable books, and were shamelessly exploited for their entertainment value on television pro-grams and talk shows—even serious ones, such as CBS's *48 Hours*, then hosted by the eminent anchorman Dan Rather, and CNN's *Larry King Live*. The low point was reached by Fox TV. In 1995 the network began showing grainy black-and-white footage of what was purported to be a govern-ment autopsy of one of the aliens—a broadcast that garnered such exceptional ratings (and such exceptional advertising revenues) that it was rerun repeatedly for three years. Then, when ratings finally began to wane, Fox dramatically "ex-posed" the entire thing as a hoax.

In 1994, to the astonishment of believers and skeptics alike, a search of military records for information about the Roswell incident uncovered a still-secret government pro-gram from the 1940s called Project Mogul. There really had been a cover-up, it turned out—but not of an alien spaceship.

Project Mogul

In the summer of 1947 the U.S.S.R. had not yet detonated its first atomic bomb, but it had become clear by then that it was only a matter of time. It was imperative that the United States know about the event when it happened. A variety of ways to detect that first Soviet nuclear test were being ex-plored. Project Mogul was an attempt to "listen" for the ex-plosion with low-frequency acoustic microphones flown to high altitudes in the upper atmosphere. The idea was not en-tirely harebrained: the interface between the troposphere and the stratosphere creates an acoustic channel through which sound waves can propagate around the globe. Acoustic sensors, radar tracking reflectors and other equipment were sent aloft on long trains of weather balloons, in the hope that they would be able to pick up the sound of an atomic explosion.

The balloon trains were launched from Alamogordo, New Mexico, about a hundred miles west of Roswell. One of the surviving scientists from Project Mogul, the physicist Charles B. Moore, professor emeritus at the New Mexico Institute of Mining and Technology in Socorro, recalls that Flight 4, launched on June 4, 1947, was tracked to within seventeen miles of the spot where Brazel found wreckage ten days later. Then, Moore says, contact was lost. The debris found on the Foster Ranch closely matched the materials used in the balloon trains. The Air Force now concludes that it was, beyond any reasonable doubt, the crash of Flight 4 that set off the bizarre series of events known as the Roswell incident. Had Project Mogul not been highly secret, unknown even to the military authorities in Roswell, the entire episode would probably have ended in July 1947. . . .

By 1997 the Air Force had collected every scrap of information dealing with the Roswell incident into a massive report, in hopes of bringing the story to an end. . . . Responding to requests from self-appointed UFO investigators acting under the Freedom of Information Act had become a heavy burden on the Air Force staff at the Pentagon, and they were eager to get ahead of the Roswell incident. The release of *The Roswell Report: Case Closed* drew one of the largest crowds on record for a Pentagon press conference.

Although the people involved insist that it was mere coincidence, the Air Force report was completed just in time for the fiftieth anniversary of Brazel's discovery of the Project Mogul wreckage. Thousands of UFO enthusiasts descended on Roswell, now a popular tourist destination, in July 1997 for a golden-anniversary celebration. They bought alien dolls and commemorative T-shirts, and snatched up every book they could find on UFOs and aliens. The only book that sold poorly was the Air Force report.

The Too-Late Truth

If there is any mystery still surrounding the Roswell incident, it is why uncovering Project Mogul in the 1990s failed to put an end to the UFO myth. Several reasons seem plausible, and they are all related to the fact that the truth came out almost half a century too late. The disclosures about Project Mogul were pounced on by UFO believers as proof that everything the government had said before was a lie. What reason was there to think that Project Mogul was not just another one?

Furthermore, Project Mogul was not the only secret government program that bolstered belief in UFOs. During the cold war, U-2 spy planes often flew over the Soviet Union. At first, U-2s were silver-colored, and their shiny skins strongly reflected sunlight, making them highly visible—particularly in the morning and evening, when the surface below was dark. In fact, the CIA estimates that more than half of all the UFO reports from the late 1950s and throughout the 1960s were actually sightings of secret U-2 reconnaissance flights. To allay public concerns at the time, the Air Force concocted far-fetched explanations involving natural phenomena. Keeping secrets, as most people learn early in life, inevitably leads to telling lies.

But secrecy, it seems, is an integral part of military culture, and it has generated a mountain of classified material. No one really knows the size of that mountain, and despite periodic efforts at reform, more classified documents exist today than there were at the height of the cold war. The government estimates that the direct cost of maintaining those records is about $3.4 billion per year, but the true cost—in loss of credibility for the government—is immeasurable. In a desperate attempt to bring the system under control, in 1995 President Bill Clinton issued an executive order that will automatically declassify documents that are more than twenty-five years old—estimated at well in excess of a billion pages—beginning in the year 2000.

Recent polls indicate that a growing number of people think the government is covering up information about UFOs. Nevertheless, it is easy to read too much significance into reports of widespread public belief in alien visits to earth. The late astronomer and science popularizer Carl Sagan saw in the myth of the space alien the modern equivalent of the demons that haunted medieval society, and for a susceptible few they are a frightening reality. But for most people, UFOs and aliens merely add a touch of excitement and mystery to uneventful lives. They also provide a handy way for people to thumb their noses at the government.

The real cost of the Roswell incident must be measured in terms of the erosion of public trust. In the interests of security, people in every society must grant their governments a license to keep secrets, and in times of perceived national danger, that license is broadened. It is a perilous bargain. A curtain of official secrecy can conceal waste, corruption and foolishness, and information can be selectively leaked for political advantage. That is a convenient arrangement for government officials, but in the long run, as the Roswell episode teaches, it often backfires. Secrets and lies leave the government powerless to reassure its citizens in the face of far-fetched conspiracy theories. Concealment is the soil in which pseudoscience flourishes.

Periodical Bibliography

The following articles have been selected to supplement the diverse views presented in this chapter.

Loyd Auerbach — "Psychic Frontiers," *Fate*, February 1999.

Susan Blackmore — "What Can the Paranormal Teach Us About Consciousness?" *Skeptical Inquirer*, March 2001.

S. Carpenter — "ESP Findings Send Controversial Message," *Science News*, July 31, 1999.

John H. Ingersoll — "Haunted Houses," *Country Living*, October 1997.

Randolph W. Liebeck — "Going After Ghosts?: A Ghostbuster's Toolkit," *Fate*, April 1997.

Scott O. Lilienfeld — "New Analyses Raise Doubts About Replicability of ESP Findings," *Skeptical Inquirer*, November 1999.

Craig Miller — "Seeing Beyond," *Fate*, March 1998.

Joe Nickell — "Alien Implants: The New 'Hard Evidence,'" *Skeptical Inquirer*, September/October 1998.

Joe Nickell — "Investigating Spirit Communications," *Skeptical Briefs*, September 1998.

Todd C. Riniolo and Louis A. Schmidt — "Testing Psi and Psi-Missing," *Skeptic* (Altadena, CA), Fall 1999.

Michael Shermer — "We See What We Believe We See," *Los Angeles Times*, June 26, 1997.

Scott S. Smith — "Leap of Faith," *Fate*, April 1999.

Keith Thompson — "Crop Circles: Stalking a Grain of Truth," *IONS Noetic Science Review*, April–July 1999.

Joy Ufema — "Sprited Encounters," *Nursing*, April 2001.

Jim Wilson — "A Dummy Explanation," *Popular Mechanics*, September 1997.

Philip Yancey — "Beyond Flesh and Blood," *Christianity Today*, April 2, 2001.

CHAPTER 3

Are UFOs Extraterrestrial Spacecraft?

Chapter Preface

One of the most intriguing claims among believers in para-normal phenomena is the allegation that extraterrestrial spacecraft are visiting the Earth. According to various polls taken in the late 1990s, between 30 and 50 percent of Americans are convinced that unidentified flying objects (UFOs) are alien spacecraft. Their beliefs are often based on the accounts of credible eyewitnesses who claim to have seen unusual objects that defy the laws of ordinary physics, moving in ways that no manmade aircraft could move. Moreover, some UFO reports are bolstered by persuasive photographs and films of odd-looking objects that hover, zigzag, or fly away at incredible speeds.

One event that some believe offers proof of the existence of alien spacecraft is the "Phoenix lights" incident of 1997. On March 13, between 7:30 and 10:30 in the evening, thousands of Phoenix-area residents observed a large arc of six lights floating over an area northwest of the city. These lights were captured on video and shown on many news stations across the nation. Some witnesses—among them teachers, law-enforcement officers, and physicians—also reported seeing a huge, dark, boomerang-shaped craft silently gliding overhead. Eyewitness Tim Ley reported that he and his family watched as the arc of lights passed a mere 100 feet over their house, when they were able to see it as a "dark shape with immense lights in it" that blocked out the stars. Many observers were astounded by the object's apparent size—ostensibly the length of twenty-five airliners.

Skeptics view the "Phoenix lights" UFO incident as a classic example of perceptual error. According to debunker Robert Sheaffer, the image of several bright lights in a row

> was in fact a [military] flare drop occurring at 9:57 P.M. from eight aircraft of the 175th Maryland Air National Guard on a training mission over the Barry Goldwater Gunnery Range. The planes were dropping high-intensity flares from 15,000 feet, which fall slowly by parachute, illuminating the target area. . . . Very likely, this was a training mission in night refueling.

Sheaffer's explanation is supported by several people who

were at Phoenix's Sky Harbor Airport that night, who claimed that they saw smoke emanating from bright flares. Furthermore, researcher Kenny Young maintains that there is no proof that the lights were part of an immense craft. He argues that the reports of a large V-shaped object were the result of "honest visual misinterpretation on the part of the confused observer."

The "Phoenix lights" incident is a definitive example of the ongoing debate between skeptics and believers in the paranormal. While skeptics seek out mundane explanations for seemingly bizarre occurrences, many believers rely on the accounts of trustworthy eyewitnesses to support their hypotheses about the improbable. Critics of the skeptical interpretation of the Phoenix event, for example, point out that many people reported seeing the lights at 7:30 P.M.—ninety minutes *before* the military flares were supposed to have been dropped. Skeptics, however, maintain that these individuals were simply mistaken about what time it was.

In the following chapter, supporters and doubters of the extraterrestrial theory offer further discussion on the question of unidentified flying objects.

"The fact that life emerged on Earth suggests that it exists in other parts of the cosmos."

Intelligent Life May Exist on Other Planets

Clifford A. Pickover

Life probably exists on other worlds, maintains Clifford A. Pickover in the following viewpoint. Because the universe is affected by the same physical and chemical forces that brought about life on Earth, it is likely that other planets have simple—and possibly even complex—life forms. The author speculates that the discovery of extraterrestrial intelligence would have a profound impact on society because human life would come to be seen as part of a larger cosmic design. Pickover is the author of several books and articles on science, art, and mathematics, including *The Science of Aliens*, from which this viewpoint is excerpted.

As you read, consider the following questions:
1. What fact leads Pickover to conclude that the development of life is easy?
2. Where might humans first find extraterrestrial life, in the author's opinion?
3. In Pickover's view, why should SETI (the Search for Extraterrestrial Intelligence) be funded?

Once He created the Big Bang . . . He could have envisioned it going in billions of directions as it evolved, including billions of life-forms and billions of kinds of intelligent beings. As a theologian, I would say that the proposed search for extraterrestrial intelligence [SETI] is also a search of knowing and understanding God through his works—especially those works that most reflect Him. Finding others than ourselves would mean knowing Him better.

—Theodore M. Hesburgh, C.S.C.,
University of Notre Dame

Our present world would certainly be mind-boggling to most people of any previous century. The one constant today is change itself. By facing and anticipating change, we can dilute fear of the unknown and act in ways that are most appropriate for both ourselves and society at large.

—Edward Cornish

Is mankind alone in the universe? Or are there somewhere other intelligent beings looking up into their night sky from very different worlds and asking the same kind of question?

—Carl Sagan and Frank Drake, *Cosmology+1.*

S omeday in the not-too-distant future we will find life on other worlds. The fact that life emerged on Earth suggests that it exists in other parts of the cosmos because the elements of which the entire universe is composed are remarkably uniform. If some of the elements have combined similar ways elsewhere, we have every reason to believe that there are other water-rich worlds in the universe with complex organic molecules. This means that there should be many worlds in the Milky Way capable of supporting simple life-forms. Even as you read these words, there must be planets in other galaxies on which life is just emerging or even flourishing. Just as you blink, some new life-form is arising.

Life emerged extremely quickly on Earth. Indeed, life arose just as soon as it possibly could. From this we can conclude that the development of life is easy. Given sufficient time and the proper environment, life will emerge through the inexorable force of the laws of physics and chemistry. Perhaps early stages of life on some planets may not be wildly different from the first one-celled organisms on Earth. Of course, the complex multicelled aliens that may evolve would be very different from us, having followed their own complex and chaotic evolutionary path. Even if our universe turns out to only permit life based on carbon, such a condition places little limitation on what form life may take. For example, on Earth carbon constitutes everything from a beautiful rose to ten-foot-long sulfur-eating worms at the bottom of the ocean.

Altering Humanity's Worldview

I believe that the definitive discovery of alien microbes on a water world like Europa would drastically alter our worldview and change our society as profoundly as did the Copernican, Darwinian, and Einsteinian revolutions—particularly if the alien microbe could be shown to have evolved independently of Earth. It would impact religious thought and spur interest in science as never before.

Some religious thinkers seem to believe that attempts to create "life" in a test tube are wrong and against the will of God. Yet we have seen that life is built into the chemistry of the universe, poised to evolve wherever conditions are right. If we discover *advanced* life-forms in the universe, far from demoting humanity to the status of inferior creatures, this discovery would give us reason to believe that we are part of a grander process of cosmic organization and hope.

If intelligent space-faring aliens evolved and we were able to communicate with them, our correspondence could bring us a richer treasure of information than medieval Europe inherited from ancient Greeks like Plato and Aristotle. Just imagine the rewards of learning alien languages, music, art, mythology, philosophy, biology, and even politics. Who would be the aliens' mythical heroes? Are their gods more like the thundering Zeus and Yaweh, or the gentler Jesus and Baha'u'llah?

During our Renaissance, rediscovered ancient texts and new knowledge flooded medieval Europe with the light of intellectual transformation, wonder, creativity, exploration, and experimentation. Another, even more exciting, Renaissance would be fueled by the wealth of alien scientific, technical and sociological information. Interestingly, the spirit of our Renaissance achieved its sharpest formulation in art. Art came to be seen as a branch of knowledge, valuable in its own right and capable of providing both spiritual and scientific images of our position in the universe. Similarly, the Renaissance caused by alien contact would transform art with new ideas, forms, and emotions.

Wouldn't it be a wild world in which to live if alien messages and technology were common—like the computer and telephone? In such a world, it might be possible to manipulate space and time in such a way as to make travel to other worlds easier. As early as Georg Bernhard Riemann (1826–1866), mathematicians have studied the properties of multiply connected spaces in which different regions of space and time are spliced together. Physicists, who once considered this an intellectual exercise for armchair speculation, are now seriously studying advanced branches of mathematics to create practical models of our universe, and to better understand the possibilities of parallel worlds and travel using wormholes and by manipulating time.

Finding Extraterrestrial Life

Where will we first find extraterrestrial life? Europa, a moon of Jupiter, seems a likely candidate because recent images reveal Europa's frosty surface to be nothing more than an ice cap floating atop an ocean of water. The *Galileo* space probe in 1997 found brown stains on the ice that could conceivably be a mix of hydrogen cyanide and other life-related chemicals. There are also stranger possibilities to consider. For example, on Jupiter's moon Io and on Venus, life might exist in liquid sulfur. Though Io appears dehydrated, planetologists don't rule out the possibility of subsurface water. Neptune's moon Triton, although quite cold, appears heavy with subsurface ice that was once sufficiently warm to flow over the landscape. Dark streaks near the poles suggest that occasional geysering spouted carbon or some other organic material. Saturn's Titan, larger than both Mercury and Pluto, has an atmosphere 60 percent denser than Earth's and forms a photochemical haze filled with prebiological chemicals. Although we expect Titan to be quite cold, it is an ideal location to check for ammonia- or hydrocarbon-based life.

Various astrophysicists have speculated wildly on life based entirely on different physical processes including plasma life within stars (based on the reciprocal influence of magnetic force patterns and the ordered motion of charged particles); life in solid hydrogen (based on ortho- and para-hydrogen molecules); radiant life (based on ordered patterns of radiation); and life in neutron stars (based on polymer chains storing and transmitting information). It may be difficult to think of these physical processes as being alive and able to organize into complex behaviors, societies, and civilizations. However, when viewed from afar, it is equally hard to imagine that interactions between proteins and nucleic acids could possibly lead to the wondrous panoply and complexity of Earthly life—from majestic blue whales and ancient redwoods to curious, creative humans who study the stars. If you were a silicon alien from another star system, and you had a map of human DNA or a list of our amino acids, could you use it to predict the rise of civilization? Could you have imagined a mossy cavern, a black viper, a retina, a seagull's cry, or the tears of a little girl? Would you have foreseen Beethoven, Einstein, Michelangelo, or Jesus?

What Might Be

Some of you may be wondering why seasoned scientists are interested in inventing and discussing hypothetical alien life-forms. Science works by asking questions and wondering what *might* be. This is the way scientists devise theories and test hypotheses. Scientific science fiction, such as Carl Sagan's *Contact*, teaches the public how science is done and why it should be supported. It teaches us to wonder about the awesome scale of our universe. Science fiction stories about space travel have already inspired humans to travel to the moon. Similarly, stories about aliens inspire us to learn more about life's chemistry and to create new radio listening devices seeking signs of extraterrestrial life. Will space travel stories inspire us to create increasingly potent technology to travel farther in the universe? Will we ever find a way to overcome the Einstein speed limit and make all of space-time our home?

Zen Buddhists have developed questions and statements called *koans* that function as a meditative discipline. Koans ready the mind so that it can entertain new intuitions, perceptions, and ideas. Koans can not be answered in ordinary ways because they are paradoxical; they function as tools for enlightenment because they jar the mind. Similarly, the contemplation of alien life is replete with koans, and that is why this Conclusion poses more questions than it answers. These questions are koans for scientific minds.

The Possibility of Alien Civilizations

In August 2000, astronomers were greatly excited by the news that 12, or maybe 13, new planets had been discovered, bringing to more than 60 the number of planets known to be circling stars in the galaxy. Most of them, of course, are huge gaseous worlds such as Jupiter and seem totally inhospitable to life. These are the only planets known to us because we don't yet have the technology to find smaller alien worlds.

But the time will come, perhaps within decades, when we will have telescopes capable of finding thousands of planets the size of Earth. Some may prove to be worlds at suitable distances from their parent suns—neither too hot nor too cold—on which advanced civilisations may have evolved.

Adrian Berry, *Spectator*, September 2000.

I wonder what humanity will discover as it searches for extraterrestrial life during the next century or two. How far will we travel? Around 4 billion years ago, living creatures on Earth were nothing more than biochemical machines capable of self-reproduction. In a mere fraction of this time, humans evolved from creatures like Australopithecines. Today humans have wandered the Moon and have studied ideas ranging from general relativity to quantum cosmology. Who knows what beings we will evolve into? Who knows what intelligent machines we will create that will be our ultimate heirs? These creatures might survive virtually forever, and our ideas, hopes, and dreams may be carried with them. There is a strangeness to the cosmic symphony that may encompass time travel, higher dimensions, quantum superspace, and parallel universes—worlds that resemble our own and perhaps even occupy the same space as our own in some ghostly manner. The astrophysicist Stephen Hawking has even proposed using wormholes to connect our universe with an *infinite* number of parallel universes. The theoretical physicist Edward Witten is working hard on superstring theory, which has already created a sensation in the world of physics because it can explain the nature of both matter and space-time. Our heirs, whatever or whoever they may be, will explore alien worlds to degrees we cannot currently fathom. They will discover that the universe is a symphony of life-forms played in many keys. There are infinite harmonies to be explored.

Funding SETI

I believe that SETI, the search for extraterrestrial intelligence, is important and should be funded, even if there is only a slight chance of detecting an extraterrestrial signal. Aside from advancing our knowledge of computer technology, radio astronomy, communication, chemistry, and biology, SETI is among the wildest adventures in human history. It is our nature to dream, to search, and to wonder about our place in a seemingly lonely cosmos. I agree with Eric Fromm, who wrote in *The Art of Loving*, "The deepest need of man is to overcome his separateness, to leave the prison of his aloneness."

"A galaxy brimming with intelligent life is very unlikely."

The Existence of Intelligent Life on Other Planets Is Unlikely

Mark Wolverton

Recent scientific inquiry suggests that the possibility of intelligent extraterrestrial life is remote, writes Mark Wolverton in the following viewpoint. While simple life forms may be relatively common on other planets, the emergence of complex life depends on several factors, including a planet's distance from its sun, climate, geological forces, and the effects of moons and other objects in the solar system. The odds that all such factors will converge in a way that allows the development of complex organisms are extremely poor, Wolverton explains. So far, Earth appears to be the only planet where all the conditions necessary to sustain complex life are present. Wolverton is a freelance science writer.

As you read, consider the following questions:

1. According to scientists Peter Ward and Donald Brownlee, cited by the author, what is the Rare Earth Hypothesis?
2. How might plate tectonics affect evolution, according to the author?
3. In what way might humanity benefit from the recognition that extraterrestrial intelligence is unlikely, according to Wolverton?

It's all the fault of Copernicus, Galileo, and Darwin. Once they proved that we humans aren't the center of the cosmos, they made it possible for the idea of extraterrestrial intelligence to become an article of pop-cultural faith. The argument usually boils down to a probability game: the basic elements of life are common in the universe and easily form organic molecules, and with so many stars and so many galaxies, the odds in favor of extraterrestial (ET) life seem overwhelming. And not just life: intelligent life. It couldn't be just us in all that vastness, could it? Of course not. The idea is beneath consideration.

But geologist Peter Ward and astronomer Donald Brownlee do consider it in their book *Rare Earth*, raising a host of troubling questions that even the most zealous extraterrestrial intelligence (ETI) proponent will find difficult to ignore. After forty years of intermittent Search for Extraterrestrial Intelligence (SETI) searches with nary a peep from the cosmos, coupled with paradigm-shattering discoveries in evolutionary biology and geology; the scientific consensus is changing. It is a game of chance—but the odds for ETI are worse than we think.

The Rare Earth Hypothesis

It's not an easy idea to accept. More examples of "extremophiles," organisms existing under the most seemingly hostile conditions, turn up in the journals every year. If life can exist and thrive in frozen Antarctic lakes, deep-ocean volcanic vents, even inside nuclear reactors, why can't it exist on other planets?

The reason, as Brownlee and Ward explain, is that there's a huge difference between simple life and complex life. The gulf between the simplest self-replicating organic molecules that could be called alive, and the immense complexity of metazoans (i.e., multicellular animals) is vast. It's this gulf that forms the basis of the "Rare Earth Hypothesis": "the paradox that life may be nearly everywhere but complex life almost nowhere." By tracing the best (and so far, only) example we have—the evolution of life on Earth—Brownlee and Ward show that the path from simplicity to complexity is not a straight line, not an inevitable journey, and fraught with so many dangers and dead ends that it's a marvel that human beings exist to wonder at the process.

Rare Earth lays out a series of factors that appear to be crucial to the development of complex life. Some have been known for years, such as the necessity of a planet being the right distance from its sun (like Goldilocks's soup, not too hot and not too cold), a stable planetary environment, and the absence of any threatening nearby astronomical phenomena to scald the planet with radiation. Others, however, have only been recently recognized. The spectacular 1994 impact of Comet Shoemaker-Levy-9 with Jupiter made abundantly clear the role that Jupiter plays in protecting us from cosmic catastrophe: the planet acts as a gravitational vacuum cleaner, sucking up incoming debris and preventing it from reaching the inner Solar System. Without Jupiter, life on Earth might have been obliterated long before ever gaining a secure foothold.

Somerville. © 1998 by *Nexus*. Reprinted with permission.

Some factors are more local in scope. The presence of a large moon helps to stabilize Earth's axial tilt and slow its rotation, keeping climactic variations in check. Geology is also a crucial consideration. One of *Rare Earth*'s most fascinating ideas is the importance that plate tectonics might have played in the evolution of animals. By creating mountains, deserts, lakes, and all the other myriad varieties of microenvironments on Earth, plate tectonics encouraged the process of speciation—the development of different types of organisms capable of surviving in a greater range of conditions. The advantage? More chance of at least some form of complex life surviving later planetary catastrophes. It's already happened. The dinosaurs weren't able to survive the conditions after the impact event that occurred sixty millions years ago—but if the small mammalian creatures arising at that time hadn't been able to adapt, we wouldn't be here today. The heat and movement of the planetary core that drive plate tectonics also create Earth's magnetic field, shielding its surface from lethal radiation.

Complex Life Is Delicate

What are the chances of all the necessary factors coming together to allow the emergence of complex organisms? Not good, unfortunately. As far as we know, it's only happened once. And planetary catastrophes capable of wiping out life happen fairly frequently (in a geological sense at least). Brownlee and Ward describe ten separate mass extinction events that have been recorded on Earth, and many more may have occurred. Each time, some remnant of life has been able to hang on and keep the story going, but there are no guarantees. The continued existence and evolution of complex life is a fine and delicate daisy chain, capable of being broken at any point, and the longer it goes on, the greater the odds against it become.

Frankly, for those of us who have dreamed of great interstellar civilizations and encounters with other intelligences, it's all pretty depressing. But *Rare Earth* isn't trying to maliciously spoil our party. It's just trying to bring our expectations more in line with what increasingly seems to be the way things are. Brownlee and Ward argue that simple life may be even more common in the universe than is currently believed. But a galaxy brimming with intelligent life is very unlikely. They may be out there, somewhere; if not in this galaxy, perhaps others. If Brownlee and Ward are right, however, we will probably never be able to meet them or communicate with them.

Yet there may be a sort of inadvertent benefit. Humanity may be more special than it seems. As Brownlee and Ward put it: "We are not the center of the universe, and we never will be. But we are not so ordinary as Western science has made us out to be for two millennia. Our global inferiority complex may be unwarranted."

I still hope they're out there somewhere, and I still run "SETI@home" on my computer, and I still get excited whenever there's talk of life on Mars or Titan. But if we really are alone, maybe it won't be so bad if that realization helps us to truly value and cherish our own precious existence in the universe.

| "Planets, stars, fireballs, birds, and the moon—all have been commonly mistaken for extraterrestrial spacecraft."

Most UFOs Are Natural or Manmade Phenomena

Philip J. Klass

Philip J. Klass, a science writer and UFO investigator, is the author of *UFOs: The Public Deceived* and *The REAL Roswell Crashed Saucer Coverup*. In the following viewpoint, Klass argues that most UFOs are really MPOs—Misidentified Prosaic Objects—such as planets, meteors, or aircraft. Observers can be tricked by their own minds and easily mistake ordinary objects for flying saucers, he points out. Even UFO sightings that are classified as "unexplainable" are likely the result of hoaxes or fantasy. Moreover, Klass maintains, when no explanation can be found for certain sightings, people should not jump to the conclusion that alien spacecraft exist.

As you read, consider the following questions:
1. According to Klass, what sort of "evidence" is typically collected at alleged UFO landing sites?
2. In the author's opinion, what might account for UFO sightings in which an object appears to follow a driver in his or her car?
3. Beyond planets, the moon, and space debris, what other kinds of objects can trigger UFO reports, according to Klass?

P lanets, stars, fireballs, birds, and the moon—all have been commonly mistaken for extraterrestial spacecraft.

Despite widespread media coverage of UFOs (Unidentified Flying Objects), one important and well-demonstrated fact is seldom mentioned: At least 90 percent of all UFOs are really "Misidentified Prosaic Objects," or MPOs. More than one-third of all UFO reports are generated by bright planets, stars, meteorfireballs, and even, occasionally by the moon.

For example, the March 20, 1975, edition of the Yakima, Washington *Herald-Republic* carried a front page feature stating that three credible local citizens reported seeing a bright UFO in the western sky around 9 P.M. and watched it for about 45 minutes "until it disappeared." One man, who described the UFO as being cone-shaped with a "greenish bluish light at the top and a sort of pale flame light at the bottom," said he had never seen anything like it before. Not surprisingly, the front-page story prompted other Yakima citizens to look for a UFO that night.

The next day's edition reported that many more persons had called in to report seeing the UFO, which had returned to the western sky that night at about the same time. The following day, the newspaper reported that its staff had been "swamped by calls by people mystified and convinced they were seeing an alien craft from outer space."

Fortuitously, one of the callers was an amateur astronomer who, after reading the two previous newspaper articles, had decided to take a look at the UFO. He reported it was the then bright planet Venus. Commendably, the *Herald-Republic* reported the UFO's identification on its front page, whereas many newspapers would have buried the explanation at the bottom of page 18.

No Proof of Alien Spacecraft

There is scant scientifically credible data on the relationship between MPOs and UFOs. Since 1969, when the U.S. Air Force formally ended its 20-plus-year investigation of UFO reports and closed down its Project Blue Book office, nearly all of the people who now investigate UFO reports want to believe that some UFOs represent visitations by extraterrestrial [ET] spacecraft.

Despite many reports of UFO landings and persons who claim to have been abducted and taken aboard a flying saucer, no one has yet come up with a single credible physical artifact to confirm the ET hypothesis. The "physical evidence" found at alleged UFO landing sites typically consists of broken tree branches, or small holes that could be the work of wild animals, or a hoaxer. Not one of the many so-called "abductees" has come back with an ET souvenir or any new ET scientific information which could be verified to confirm their tale.

Because nearly half a century of UFO investigation has failed to yield a single, scientifically credible physical artifact, the only evidence supporting the ET hypothesis rests entirely on "unexplained" UFO cases. If an investigator is unable to find a prosaic explanation for a UFO report, believers in the ET hypothesis cite this as evidence that the UFO report was generated by an ET craft.

Because nearly all of the persons who now investigate UFO reports are eager to find "unexplainable" cases, this gives them scant incentive to conduct a rigorous investigation of a tough case. During my more than 30 years of investigating UFO reports, several cases required many months of part-time effort to find a prosaic explanation and one required more than two years.

Allan Hendry and CUFOS

A notable exception is the UFO investigative work of Allan Hendry, who became the chief investigator for the Center for UFO Studies (CUFOS), shortly after he graduated from the University of Michigan in 1972 with a B.A. in astronomy and illustration. CUFOS had just been created by J. Allen Hynek, who then headed Northwestern University's astronomy department.

In the late 1940s, the Air Force hired Hynek as a consultant after it discovered that bright celestial bodies generated many UFO reports and that even experienced military pilots sometimes chased after a UFO that turned out to be a bright planet or star. At the time, Hynek was teaching astronomy at Ohio State University—not far from the Project Blue Book offices in Dayton. In 1969, when the Air Force decided to close down Project Blue Book, it terminated Hynek's contract. Several years later he created CUFOS and hired Hendry as its full-time UFO investigator.

For Hendry, with a long-standing interest in UFOs, it was an exciting opportunity. Although Hynek had been a hard-nosed skeptic about the ET hypothesis when he was first hired by Project Blue Book, in his later years he became more "open-minded." He hoped that CUFOS could conduct a competent scientific investigation into the UFO mystery. To encourage UFO reports by law enforcement officers, who were considered to be more reliable than the general public, CUFOS obtained a toll-free 800 telephone line whose number was given to many police departments.

During the next 15 months, Hendry personally investigated 1,307 UFO reports submitted to CUFOS—many more cases than any other investigator up to that time, or since. The results were published in 1979 by Doubleday/Dolphin in a book entitled *The UFO Handbook: A Guide to Investigating, Evaluating and Reporting UFO Sightings.*

Hendry's book—regrettably long out of print—provides the most recent scientifically credible data on the many different "trigger mechanisms" which generate UFO reports. Earlier Project Blue Book data is criticized by some who charge that the Air Force's eagerness to explain away UFO reports resulted in unrealistic explanations. Hendry's data is not vulnerable to such charges because he admitted he would like to find evidence that some UFOs were ET craft.

Of the 1,307 UFO cases that Hendry investigated, he found prosaic explanations for 91.4 percent of them, leaving 113, or 8.6 percent, unexplained. However, Hendry conceded that 93 of these 113 unexplained reports had possible prosaic explanations. This left only 20 cases, or 1.5 percent of the total, as seemingly unexplainable in prosaic terms. Is that evidence that some or all of these 20 unexplained cases involved ET spacecraft?

Hendry wisely resisted making any such claim. In the closing pages of his book, he admitted that rigorous investigation alone is not always sufficient to find a prosaic explanation, which sometimes depends on "sheer luck." (Based on my own investigations over the past 30 years, I fully agree.)

Another factor, which Hendry does not mention, is that with his other CUFOS duties, which included producing a monthly publication for subscribers, he could spend an average of only two hours in his investigation of each case. Some of the cases I have investigated have required many dozens or hundreds of hours of effort to find a prosaic explanation.

What About the "Unexplained" Cases?

Early in my own career as a UFO investigator, I was "taken in" by several hoaxers who seemed at first to be honest. I suspect that at least several of Hendry's "unexplainable" cases are hoaxes and that he was too trusting, as I had been.

In the concluding pages of Hendry's book, he commented: "How can I be sure if my remaining 'UFOs' aren't simply Identified Flying Objects [i.e., Misidentified Prosaic Objects] misperceived (sincerely) to the point of fantasy? The emotional climate about the subject (as revealed by Identified Flying Objects) appears to be adequate to support such a hypothesis for a great many UFO situations, if not all. . . . With our current inability to fully draw the distinction between real UFOs and IFOs, fantasies or hoaxes, coupled with a heated emotional atmosphere, I can only assert that it is my feeling that some UFO reports represent truly remarkable events." But Hendry admitted that "while science may be initiated by feelings, it cannot be based on them."

Hendry's investigation showed that nearly 28 percent of all UFO sightings reported to CUFOS proved to be bright stars and planets. Hendry noted that UFOs that turned out to be celestial bodies were often reported to "dart up and down," to "execute loops and figure eights." Occasionally the celestial UFO was reported to "meander in square patterns" or "zigzag." In 49 cases triggered by a bright celestial body, the witnesses estimated the UFO's distance at figures ranging from 200 feet to 125 miles.

When I first entered the UFO field, I would have challenged the idea that an intelligent person could mistake a bright celestial body for a UFO that was "following them." But numerous incidents, some involving law enforcement officers, have convinced me otherwise. If a person driving in a car sees a bright celestial object ahead and suspects that it might be a UFO, and accelerates to try to get closer, no matter how fast the driver goes, he/she cannot seem to gain on the UFO. If the driver then stops and gets out of the car, the "UFO" seems to halt also, because it is getting no bigger or smaller. Now, if the driver decides to return home, the "UFO" seems to be following the car because it remains the same size and brightness.

Extraordinary Claims Require Extraordinary Evidence

The discovery that there are other intelligent beings in the universe—and, as a corollary, that life and intelligence can and has evolved at locations other than Earth—and that, moreover, these beings are visiting Earth on a semi-regular basis in spacecraft that seem to defy the laws of physics as we now know them, would unquestionably rank as the greatest discovery in the history of science, and most definitely is an extraordinary claim. Therefore, in order for me to accept it, you must produce extraordinary evidence. What might this evidence be? For one thing, the aliens themselves. Not some story where someone says that someone says that someone says that they saw aliens, but the actual physical aliens themselves, where I and other trustworthy and competent scientists and individuals can study and communicate with them. I'd like to examine their spacecraft and learn the physical principles under which it operates. I'd like a ride on that spacecraft. I'd like to see their star charts and see where the aliens come from. I'd like to know the astronomical, physical, chemical, and biological conditions of their home world and solar system, and how they compare with and contrast with ours. If possible, I'd like to visit their home world, and any other worlds that might be within their sphere of influence. In other words, I want the aliens visible front and center, where there can be *no reasonable doubt* as to their existence. Stories about "lights" or "things" in the sky do not impress me, especially when such reports come from people who have no idea of the vast array of natural and man-made phenomena that are visible in the sky if one would only take the time to look.

Alan Hale, *Skeptical Inquirer*, March/April 1997.

It might seem surprising that 22 of the UFO sightings reported to CUFOS turned out to be triggered by the moon.

Early in my career as a UFO investigator, I was challenged to explain an incident that had occurred with a Navy aircraft crew on February 10, 1951, while en route from Iceland to Newfoundland. The Project Blue Book files listed the case as "unexplained." After careful study of the crew's report, many hours of investigation, and a bit of luck, this UFO could be identified as the upper tip of a crescent moon which was barely visible at the horizon.

Hendry's investigation showed that nearly 18 percent of all UFO reports were generated by advertising airplanes, which carry strings of lights that spell out an advertising message. When seen at an oblique angle, their strings of flashing lights are perceived as being saucer-shaped. When the pilot decides to turn off the lamps and go home, observers report that the "UFO mysteriously disappeared." . . .

Other Triggers for UFO Reports

Hendry, who retired from "UFOlogy" shortly after his book's publication and has never returned, discovered there are many, many trigger mechanisms for UFO reports besides bright planets, fireballs, reentering space debris, and the moon. These included hoax hot air balloons, weather and scientific balloons, missile launches, birds, and kites, to cite but a few.

Several years ago, shortly before I was to give a UFO lecture to the Seattle chapter of the Institute of Electrical and Electronics Engineers, I was standing outside the lecture hall chatting with several attendees. Suddenly, one of them pointed skyward and said, "What's that?" I looked up and there was a small, orange object which seemed to be hovering at an altitude of several thousand feet.

Someone said: "It looks like a kite." I responded: "No, it's much too high to be a kite, maybe it's a weather balloon reflecting the nearly setting sun." The other party responded: "It can't be a balloon, it's not moving." Suddenly, a third man spoke up: "I think I have some binoculars in my car," and he hurried to get them. He returned with the binoculars, took a brief look and said: "It's a kite." When I viewed the UFO through the binoculars, I agreed.

Were it not for the happenstance that this man had a set

of binoculars, I would have to admit that I saw a "UFO" in Seattle that appeared to be too high to be a kite and too stationary to be a weather balloon. But it was not doing anything extraordinary—or extraterrestrial.

For 45 years I have been writing for *Aviation Week & Space Technology* magazine—for 34 years as one of its senior editors and since my "active-retirement" in 1986, as a contributing editor. The magazine has published more articles on space travel than any other publication in the world. I can think of no more exciting story it could publish, or that I could write, than to be able to report that I have finally found a UFO case that defies any possible prosaic explanation. I would expect to win a Pulitzer Prize, a giant bonus, and great fame. So far, I've had no luck. But who knows, perhaps tomorrow—or next week.

"[Skeptics argue that] since there are no UFOs, nobody could ever see one. File that under faith, not science."

Some UFOs May Be Extraterrestrial Spacecraft

Greg Sandow

In the following viewpoint, investigative journalist Greg Sandow suggests that some UFOs may be extraterrestrial spacecraft. Although most UFO reports are the result of natural phenomena, such as meteors or manmade aircraft, some sightings by credible individuals defy easy classification, writes Sandow. The issue is further complicated by the fact that the media confuses the public with misinformation. Skeptics believe that alien spacecraft cannot exist, and therefore claim that UFOs are easily explainable as hoaxes or misperceived natural phenomena, but such beliefs are no more scientific than other types of faith. While there is no conclusive proof that UFOs are extraterrestrial, those seeking to uncover the truth should remain open to all possibilities, contends Sandow.

As you read, consider the following questions:

1. What should investigators do to understand the UFO phenomenon, in Sandow's opinion?
2. According to the author, what elementary mistakes do psychologists who write about alien abduction make?
3. What is the "one firm conclusion" that Sandow is left with after four years of UFO research?

When I tell people I've done UFO research, they react in many ways, most of them interested and sympathetic. But often they ask an irresistible question. Have I heard any crazy stories?

Of course I have. How about the guy who told me aliens put a chip in his head that made women flock to him? Even better, he said, the aliens told him to go out and *use* it . . . which, I have to say, I saw him doing, though I doubt that aliens were responsible.

And then there was the woman from the Center for the Study of Extraterrestrial Intelligence (CSETI), an organization that claims to be serious and responsible but also says it's made direct contact with aliens. Its members have gone out at night, they say, blinked searchlights at the sky—and sure enough, the aliens blinked back! But when I asked if I could see this for myself, their spokeswoman turned me down, big-time. My mistake, apparently, was asking to observe as a journalist. "Oh, no," the CSETI representative replied. "We've learned our lesson. We invited CBS, and they said it didn't happen."

Then she told me that the government was beaming harmful rays at her.

The Sane Stories

But amusing as all this is—I could tell crazy UFO tales all day long—it's not the crazy stories that matter. It's the sane ones. To understand the UFO phenomenon, you need to hear firsthand accounts, from reasonable people who aren't looking for publicity, like the woman in her twenties and the older married couple, who—in separate incidents—told me they saw something really huge pass overhead in silence, flying low, at treetop height, some years ago in the Hudson Valley (an area with many reports of such sightings).

All three people described what seemed like similar patterns of metallic piping on the bottom of what they say they saw. It's that last detail that makes these sightings more than usually impressive, though I'm not going to say that these people saw spaceships. How could I? How can any of us know for sure?

But unless they're lying, it seems that they saw *something* that doesn't sound much like a weather balloon, the planet Venus, or a plane, to name a few things often blamed for UFO reports. Nor does it seem like a group of ultralight aircraft flying in formation, the explanation most commonly suggested for the Hudson Valley sightings. It's true, of course, that people often make mistakes about what they think they see. But these people insist they saw real objects that darkened the sky and had a textured underside.

You'll also find sane reports from people who think they've been abducted by aliens. Budd Hopkins, a New York painter and sculptor who's America's most famous abduction researcher, at one point invited me to look through his unopened mail.

A very few letters came from evidently crazy people. ("The aliens visit me each Thursday.") But most were simple and sincere. These writers didn't claim to have been abducted. They did think, though, that something they couldn't explain was happening. Often they sounded terrified. For most of their lives, they wrote, they'd seen unexpected lights in their rooms at night, and beings by their beds. The beings didn't necessarily seem like aliens, but the letter writers were desperate for an explanation.

They also say their encounters left otherwise unexplained marks on their bodies. And when I've met them, I've sometimes found them saying they remember things they didn't dare to write about, like being driven by their parents to an isolated field where something like "a merry-go-round with lights" was waiting for them. What they want to know—and they ask the question warily, skeptically, thinking that they're crazy just to write or type the words—is whether abductions *might* explain what they say has been happening.

The Confusion Surrounding UFOs

Often, these abductees then get hypnotized, to recover further memories, and that's controversial. Most psychologists think hypnosis can't recover memory. But psychologists who write about abductions—and I've read just about all the papers on the subject ever published in psychology journals—make elementary mistakes. Few have ever spoken to an abductee, and yet they'll write that abductees are UFO enthusiasts (not true), who proclaim their abduction memories *only* after being hypnotized (also not true). The situation is far more complex than that, but whatever's going on, it's something nobody has yet explained.

One-Sided Dogmatists

Among explorers of the paranormal, there has long been frustration with scientists who come across as arrogant. As far back as 1961, a Brookings Institution report on the possibility of other life in outer space contained the following comment: "It has been speculated that of all groups, scientists and engineers might be the most devastated by the discovery of relatively superior creatures, since these professions are most clearly associated with the mastery of nature, rather than with the understanding and expression of man."

Laurence W. Frederick, an astronomer at the University of Virginia who helps run the Society for Scientific Exploration, a paranormal investigative group, says: "There are dogmatists on one side, mostly scientists, who won't even think about the possibility that something about the paranormal might be real. But I point to the many times scientists have overlooked things that later became dogma. Stones coming out of the sky were long said by scientists to be the result of lightning hitting rocks. But in 1804, they were identified as meteors after chemical analysis showed they were extraterrestrial."

Charles S. Clark, *CQ Researcher*, March 29, 1996.

Which brings me to the craziest—and saddest—thing I've seen in the world of UFOs, and that's the confusion surrounding the subject. Mainstream media print misinformation—not *dis*information, not deliberate lies or cover-ups, but just shoddy, unchecked data, as if UFOs were beneath contempt, and no reporter need take them seriously enough to check historical facts. More seriously, one leading investigator of the Roswell crash [the alleged 1947 UFO crash in New Mexico], Kevin Randle, once told me that no one from the mainstream media had ever looked through his files to find out why he thinks the crash was of something alien. He let me do it, and what I found was quite convincing, though lately the skeptics have the upper hand, because some leading Roswell witnesses have been caught in lies or exaggerations.

And within the field of UFO research, I've found a sad polarization. On one side, we have people blinking lights at aliens, and on the other, scientific skeptics who think they can explain even serious UFO reports but don't have a clue what they're talking about. The most astonishing example came from Donald Menzel, a Harvard astronomer who wrote three books debunking UFOs.

Menzel laughed at a report from an Anglican priest in New Guinea, who said he watched beings walking around, apparently working, in a hovering UFO for more than 20 minutes. Now, I'm not going to say this really happened; I don't have a clue. But Menzel suggested—with no evidence at all—that the priest suffered from astigmatism, and either didn't know it, or had forgotten to put on his glasses. What he saw, said Menzel, was Venus, distorted by astigmatism into an oval shape—and as for beings, those were the priest's own eyelashes!

Skepticism or Denial?

I myself spent four hours arguing with Philip Klass, the most widely published current UFO skeptic, who raged that abductees make their claims only to get on TV. That's absurd. I've met dozens of them, and they fervently protect their privacy. Only one has ever let me print his name. So I had to ask: Which abductees had Klass met? "The ones who appear with me on television," he replied without a trace of irony.

I also talked about two airline pilots who made headlines back in 1948, reporting that they'd seen an unknown craft with windows swooping past their plane one night. This, Klass writes in his 1974 book, *UFOs Explained*, was "clearly" a meteor, so "clearly," in fact, that the case must be "removed for all time from the category of 'unidentifieds.'"

But how, I asked him, could he be so sure? That the pilots *could* have seen a meteor is obvious enough, since (as Klass points out) in other cases people did imagine windows, when all they saw were random lights. But even skeptics can't cite any meteor known to fall that night in 1948, so how can Klass be certain?

"Suppose something went wrong with your PC," he rumbled, chuckling, but not quite answering my question.

"Would you suspect evil spirits, or would you call a technician?" Evidently UFOs were as improbable as ghosts to him, and as easily dismissable. But I kept probing, and finally he took a stand. "Since there is no proof that unknown craft are in the sky," he said, "I prefer a prosaic explanation." Or, in other words, since there *are* no UFOs, nobody could ever see one. File that under faith, not science.

After four years of UFO research, I'm left with only one firm conclusion. Despite years of *Star Trek*, the possibility of aliens—right here, now, on Earth among us—is so unsettling that many people, both skeptics and believers, can't talk sense about it.

"The abduction phenomenon seems to be one of a number of intrusions into our reality from other realms that are contributing to the . . . spiritual rebirth taking place in Western culture."

Humans Are Being Abducted by Aliens

John E. Mack

John E. Mack, who has conducted research on people claiming to have been abducted by alien beings, is a professor of psychiatry at Harvard Medical School and the founding director of the Program for Extraordinary Experience. In the following viewpoint, excerpted from his book, *Passport to the Cosmos*, Mack contends that the phenomenon of alien visitation is real. He claims that aliens may be entities from another dimension or spiritual realm that have come to Earth as part of a divine plan to bring about a spiritual awakening and a profound change in human consciousness. This awakening could foster a new sense of responsibility for the future of the Earth and reunite humans with their "Divine Source," he concludes.

As you read, consider the following questions:

1. In Mack's opinion, why are the aliens fascinated with human physicality?
2. What is characteristic about the trauma that abductees experience, according to the author?
3. According to Mack, what four "psychospiritual" changes do abductees go through as a result of their encounters with aliens?

Excerpted from *Passport to the Cosmos: Human Transformations and Alien Encounters*, by John E. Mack (New York: Crown Publishers, 1999). Copyright © 1999 by John E. Mack. Reprinted with permission.

To a large extent, the debate surrounding UFOs has focused on the question of whether they are real in a strictly material sense and if their existence can be proven by the methods of traditional science. Similarly, with regard to abductions, interest has centered on whether people are being taken bodily through the sky into spaceships by alien beings. These may be intriguing questions. But after nearly ten years of work with abductees, I have come to the view that these are not the most significant questions posed by the alien abduction phenomenon. Rather, the most important truths for our culture may lie in the extraordinary nature and power of the abductees' experiences, the opening that these experiences provide to other deeper dimensions of reality, and what they may mean for our culture and the human future. . . .

The alien abduction phenomenon is one among a number of manifestations—including near-death experiences, intricate crop formations [the "crop circles" that some people believe are of alien origin], apparitions of many kinds, unexplained powers of healing, and parapsychology— that are forcing us to appreciate that cosmic realities exist beyond the three-dimensional universe that has bounded our earthly existence. . . .

The Abduction Phenomenon in the Human Story

I cannot offer proof of the material reality of the abduction phenomenon. Instead, I think its principal elements and place in human history can best be pulled together as a story that is coherent, even if it contains elements that may not be consistent with the worldview in which I and others of my culture were raised. Within the structure of a story or parable, I can travel more comfortably between the literal and the symbolic, between metaphoric and material reality, between certainty and uncertainty, and between the manifest and the unseen worlds.

In saying this, I do not mean to imply that it does not matter whether abduction experiencers are referring to an actual event in the physical world; are describing subtler matters that may not be literally true in a material sense; or are even (whether they know it or not) speaking metaphorically. Where these distinctions seem important, I do try to make them. But I must confess that the more deeply I have explored this phenomenon over the past decade, the less certain I have become about when the abductees are speaking of something that happened to them literally in this material reality and when they are communicating in metaphoric language events they experienced as utterly real in a physical sense but that happened to their subtle, astral, or energetic bodies, which may be the actual locus of the sense of self. . . .

The story would go something like this. It all starts with the ultimate creative principle, which abductees call variously God, Source, Home or the One. (Abductee Greg calls it "God-Goddess-All that is.") From some primal beginning—which, according to one or another cosmology, was the work of the God force, a mysterious creation of all out of nothing, or a cosmic explosion (Big Bang) from which all matter/energy emerged out of a tiny omnipotential seed—everything we now know of as this universe came almost instantaneously into being. Perhaps, as physicist Alan Guth suggests, there may be an infinite number of such universes. Be all that as it may, afterward a sequence of evolutionary events occurred, including the creation of the planet Earth and the emergence of biological life and the human species.

Human beings, having been formed originally by the God force, retained some experience of a relationship to it. But then something else happened. We developed a consciousness, a self-awareness, different from other species in that we came to know our own mortality, that our time on this Earth was limited, and that this body at least would die. For most peoples on the planet, the sorrow associated with this inescapable fact was mitigated, at least to some degree, by the sense of a persisting connection with the Source, the potential ecstasy and fulfillment of that relationship, and the conviction that there was something—a spirit, soul, psyche, or consciousness—that was eternal and would survive the body, returning to God after its death.

Sometime during the second millennium after the birth of Christ, human beings in the West (analogous processes seem to have occurred in other parts of the world) went to work to solve the problem of the body's survival and possibly to achieve immortality in a physical rather than a spiritual sense, which had never seemed altogether certain or satisfactory to many people. Through the development of powers of observation and reason, we developed modern science, medicine, and technology, through which we have sought with considerable success to struggle with the problem of mortality, to reduce some forms of suffering, and to prolong life. The part of ourselves that is devoted to this project of survival, called initially by Freud the "ego," grew in its power and importance until most human endeavors have seemed at times to be devoted to its (the ego's) preservation.

An Evolutionary Process

Dr. John Mack has not been able to conclude from his work with abductees or, rather, experiencers, that there are discrete, different types of alien beings with either an agenda or a number of agendas. In fact, he is not even comfortable with the word "agenda." He views the UFO phenomenon as part of an evolutionary process that is inextricably linked with the problems of existence, consciousness, and self-awareness. There may be an "agenda," but Dr. Mack asked, "Whose agenda is it? Is it the aliens' agenda? Is it our agenda? Or is it God's agenda, or the Cosmos's own agenda, depending on whether or not one has a deistic or nondeistic theology?"

Michael Mannion, *Project Mindshift*, 1998.

Until perhaps the middle of the eighteenth century, people in the West—as well as the indigenous peoples of the Earth, who have never lost their connection with the Creator—experienced their advancing understanding of the material world in the context of a cosmos that was ensouled, in which God continued to inhere. But sometime in that century—perhaps in part because the methods of empirical science were also applied to studying the creative principle itself, and by these methods it could not be proven to exist—many people in Western society became in large part "secular." They lost their sense of connection with the Divine, the sacred realms, the Source, God, the Creator—or whatever other name is or was used to describe an ultimate creative principle. The universe came to consist largely of dead matter, energy, and space, and our pleasures, for the most part, became restricted to earthly emotional connections and material satisfactions.

This approach to the nature of our mortality has led to some big problems. One of our great scientific areas of success, the prolongation of physical life, has led to a staggering growth in the human population, to the point where we have become one of, if not the largest, biomass on the planet. At the same time, we have created increasingly efficient methods for taking precious, nonrenewable materials from the Earth. As a result we have begun to exceed our energy resources, and by expelling into the air, land, and water the poisonous by-products of our consumption that we have not found a way to get rid of safely, we are killing off many of the planet's life-forms.

Meanwhile, our successes in the material domain have led to improved standards of living and understandable expectations for a better life among many of the Earth's peoples, thus requiring the consumption of ever more physical goods per person and putting still more pressure on the Earth's fragile environment. This increasingly short supply of food and other precious materials has exacerbated tensions between human groups, given rise to simplistic ideologies for solving economic and political problems (communism, capitalism, fascism, and so on), and threatens to bring about the virtual extinction of life as we know it through the use of weapons of mass destruction. . . .

The Human Problem from a Cosmic Perspective

Up to this point, we are pretty much on familiar ground. But now the story moves in a direction that is strongly at odds with the worldview in which I—and, I suspect, most of my readers—were brought up. I would not even have considered what follows, had not the experiencers with whom I have worked for nearly a decade provided me with this material so consistently and clearly. Evidently what we have been doing to the Earth has not gone "unnoticed" at a higher, cosmic, or cosmic/regional level. Some sort of odd intervention seems to be occurring here. We are not, apparently, being permitted to continue on our destructive ways without some kind of "feedback."

What *sort* of feedback is occurring? Well, to begin with, no united planetary environmental balancing team has been sent in to stop us, for it seems to be God's way to leave us a lot of rope. The highest intelligence appears to respect our free will and does not try to block us directly. (How could that be done anyway?) But this does not mean no intervention is occurring. I look at what the abductees have told me and then try to put myself in the Creator's place. How might it look? Two of the kinds of entities that have been brought into being—aliens and humans—appear to be in difficulty. Each has needs that the other can fulfill, although their agendas, while intersecting, are rather different in some respects.

When it comes to the aliens, there are several types with differing properties. The little gray ones with the big eyes are reliable for what is needed here, although their methods can sometimes be thoughtless and rather crude. They are especially good at shape-shifting, disguising themselves as animal forms when this is useful. The grays have been interacting with human beings and affecting their cultures and identities, usually without their knowledge, for thousands of years. They are especially "useful" now. Other beings are more luminous or transcendent. Some, like the reptilian ones, really play rough. These can fulfill a more limited role, depending on the level of consciousness of the particular human beings that are chosen or have volunteered for this project.

The aliens seem to have lost their bodies, or at least have become less densely embodied than the human beings. Some abductees are informed that something went wrong biologically for the aliens as a result of an overstepping or technological hubris of the kind we are engaged in now on this planet, and like the angels, they long to have a body. We have countless examples of the aliens' fascination with our dense physicality, sensuality, sexuality, parental love, and the like, and their apparent desire to form a union with us both for their own purposes—to enjoy, for example, the pleasures of dense embodiment—and to produce a hybrid human/alien race. Although the aliens are not themselves gods—their behavior is sometimes anything but godlike—abductees consistently report that the beings seem closer to the Godhead than we are, acting as messengers, guardian spirits, or angels, intermediaries between us and the Divine Source.

The humans, on the other hand, have the capacity for deep and intense caring, nurturance, and physical and emotional love, but they have lost the connection with their Source and seem to be treating God's finest creation, the Earth, as a piece of private property belonging to them only. This cannot be allowed to continue. By the human/alien union, a hybrid race can be created—in what realm we do not know—that maintains the biological identity and continuity of both species, should the human race succeed in its project of destroying itself and much of the other life on the Earth. Energetically speaking, this has been a tough job of adjustment, since the aliens vibrate at a considerably higher level than the humans. Lately the human/hybrid integration seems to be going better. The aliens' superior communications technology can also be used to try to get across to this stiff-necked people what they are doing to their beautiful planet and see if that will make a difference. The alien beings can also help to raise human consciousness and bring this species back into connection with the creative principle.

Shattering the Human Worldview

For environmental education something more is needed. Spawning a lot of hybrids cannot go very far toward preserving the Earth's life if human beings remain devoted to their own egoic pursuits, if their psyches do not change. This is a very big challenge. The materialist juggernaut is loose and gaining momentum, and the only thing that can stop it is a radical change in consciousness. The human ego, especially in Western cultures, bolstered by great powers of intellectual rationalization and denial, is highly resistant to change.

This brings us to perhaps the most critical and controversial aspect of the abduction phenomenon. Many, perhaps the majority, of the experiencers find their encounters to be highly traumatic, at least until they have confronted and integrated their power and meaning. But this type of trauma has some unusual characteristics. In addition to the familiar terror and helplessness that all traumatic events have in common, the abduction experiences have two other important elements.

First, the experiences seem to be created, as if by design, to shatter (the word virtually all abductees use) the previously held idea of reality (which usually had no place for such entities) and topple the experiencer from the sense of being a member of a uniquely intelligent life-form at the peak of the Great Chain of Being. In the face of forces beyond their control, abductees are confronted with their helplessness and with the existence of intelligent beings possessing technologies and other powers far in advance of our own.

Second, as they remember or relive their experiences, abductees often realize that they have encountered intense vibratory energies, still held in the body, that have also profoundly affected their consciousness. It is difficult sometimes for them to put this change into words, but they speak of it as an "awakening," or a moving to a higher level, as a direct result of the vibrations themselves. Andrea, for example, tried to explain to us that as a result of her encounters, all of the cells of her body seemed to be vibrating differently. It felt to her as if changes had occurred deep inside her "core," which seemed to transcend blocks in her awareness. "It is so much about choice and intent, and getting really conscious," Greg wrote to me.

Spiritual Awakening

Now we seem to be coming closer to the heart of the matter. For this awakening, the heightened awareness that grows out of the ego-shattering impact of the encounters, carries with it quite consistently certain interrelated psychospiritual changes, especially if the experiencers are enabled to work through the traumatic dimension of what they feel certain has happened to them.

First, they have access to what in Western societies is called nonordinary states of consciousness, similar to the symbolic worlds of the shamans of indigenous cultures. They become aware of the great archetypes of the collective unconscious, of birth, death, and rebirth, which helps them to experience their connectedness to other beings and to the Creator or Source.

Second, as a result of this deepening and expanding of their psychological and spiritual powers (abductees will often also speak of and manifest particular psychic abilities), together with the experienced shift of their bodily vibrations, they may undergo a profound connection or reconnection with the Divine, God, Source, or whatever they may call the ultimate creative principle in the cosmos. They may become, as Karin spoke of it, "disciples to Source."

Third, they experience a heart-opening, a sense of loving connection with all living beings and creation itself, which can at times take on mystical proportions. Abductees may find God or love in the perception of *light* that is a regular part of their experiences, which they see as the source of all of creation. Karin spoke of "light with a small 'l'" and "light with a capital 'L,'" which is "literally the presence of God within everything." Sharon saw or felt "love that was coming off the light" in her bedroom. "The love was overwhelming," she exclaimed. This is consistent with the findings of Norman Don and Gilda Moura, who observed that Brazilian abduction experiencers could enter voluntarily into states of hyperarousal revealed by their brain waves to be comparable only to the states of ecstasy or *samadhi* of advanced meditators or yogis.

Fourth, abductees experience a renewed sense of the sacred and a reverence for nature. Some, like Carlos Diaz, see divine light, like an aura, surrounding each living thing. Like Carlos, they may become aware of the interconnected web of life and be viscerally, sometimes unbearably, pained by the destruction of the Earth's living forms, committing themselves to their preservation. "I've learned to go back to the natural flow of things," Isabel says, "and everything just connects the way it's supposed to be."

But a good deal more happens to the abductees during their journeys. Some develop a deep and enduring relationship with a particular alien being, usually described as more powerful than any earthly relationship, and they may speak convincingly of having an alien mate and of parenting in another dimension. The connection with the gray aliens' great black eyes may seem to draw abductees into seemingly limitless or infinite depths, where knowledge and relationship occur on a soul level.

The fundamental changes that abductees make in their

lives as they come to grasp the power and meaning of their experiences has been important in convincing me of the truth and significance of their stories, whatever their onto-logical status may be. Many give up mainstream jobs, often for less well-paying ones in the healing or other human ser-vice professions, and become active in Earth-preserving pro-jects. The change in their worldviews and core beliefs is last-ing and continues to evolve. . . .

The abduction phenomenon seems to be one of a number of intrusions into our reality from other realms that are con-tributing to the gradual (at least so far) spiritual rebirth taking place in Western culture. It seems to have something to do with the human future. Each of the principal elements of the phenomenon—the traumatic intrusions; the reality-shattering encounters; the energetic intensity; the apocalyptic ecological confrontations; the reconnection with Source; and the forging of new relationships across a dimensional divide—contributes to the *daishigyo*, the great ego death, that is marking the end of the materialist business-as-usual paradigm that has lost its compatibility with life in the world as we now know it. . . .

A Shift in Consciousness

In the end, the abduction phenomenon seems to me to be a part of the shift in consciousness that is collapsing duality and enabling us to see that we are connected beyond the Earth at a cosmic level. No common enemy will unite us, but the realization of a common Source might. Our notions of the Divine, like everything else, seem to grow along with the evolution of our consciousness. We no longer expect an Old Testament God/bully that will part the seas and bring us where we need to go. Nor is it likely that a messiah/savior will lead us into the Divine Light. . . .

The god for this time, we seem to be learning from ab-ductees and others, is more of a partner than anything else, working through and with us. Now that is *really* scary, for it places choice utterly within us. From this perspective the alien abduction phenomenon is largely an opportunity or a gift, a kind of catalyst for the evolution of consciousness in the direction of an emerging sense of responsibility for our own and the planet's future.

"[There is] no persuasive evidence against the proposition that [abductees] are either deluded or fraudulent."

Humans Are Not Being Abducted by Aliens

Samuel McCracken

In the following viewpoint, Samuel McCracken argues that there is no proof that extraterrestrial beings are abducting and performing experiments on humans. Researchers who believe such claims to be true are relying on circumstantial evidence, flawed investigative procedures, and poor logic, McCracken contends. People who claim to have been abducted by aliens are either lying or being subconsciously influenced by fanciful depictions of aliens in popular culture, he maintains. McCracken is assistant to the chancellor of Boston University.

As you read, consider the following questions:
1. According to McCracken, how did the UFO phenomenon emerge?
2. In the author's opinion, what famous historical event reveals the fallibility of sincere personal narratives?
3. In what way is the Betty and Barney Hill abduction case an example of life imitating art, according to McCracken?

Over the last 50 years, the skies of popular culture have been alight with flying saucers—disk-shaped interplanetary craft operated by small beings of vaguely humanoid (if decidedly nonstandard) physiognomy and ambivalent intentions toward us earthlings. Until comparatively recently, though, these flying objects remained a fringe phenomenon—in the sense that, generally speaking, those who took them seriously were not themselves the sorts of people likely to be taken seriously. This has begun to change.

In 1994, John E. Mack, M.D., a well-regarded professor of psychiatry at the Harvard Medical School, and the winner of a Pulitzer prize for his 1977 biography of T.E. Lawrence, published a book, *Abduction: Human Encounters with Aliens*, in which people asserting they had been kidnapped by alien creatures in spaceships were considered to be sanely reporting on actual experiences. Now, in *Passport to the Cosmos: Human Transformation and Alien Encounters*, Mack has taken another step; such alien encounters, he argues, are an expression of a large and hopeful truth about our age.

When an individual with Mack's credentials promulgates ideas normally found at the grocery checkout stand, it is worth paying heed.

The Birth of UFOs

Before World War II, interplanetary and intergalactic travel, bringing the possibility of extraterrestrial visitors to earth, was the stuff of science fiction. Although prewar cognoscenti understood that building gravity-escaping ships was a problem merely of engineering, not until Werner von Braun helped Hitler demonstrate rockets-in-being did the idea of visitors from elsewhere begin to assume plausibility.

Coincidentally, World War II also taught Americans (with the aid of books like the 1942 *What's That Plane: How to Identify American and Jap Airplanes*) to scan the skies for intrusive objects. As thousands spent their spare hours scrutinizing the heavens, it was inevitable that spotters in, say, western Kansas would report sightings that conformed to no filed flight plan and that, given geographic realities, could not be hostile aircraft. In fact if not yet in terminology, these were unidentified flying objects (UFO's).

After the war, the government turned its attention to such continued sightings, identifying nine out of ten as mundane entities like helicopters or weather balloons. But that left 10 percent, some of them reputedly saucer-shaped spacecraft manned by little green (later to become gray) men. Perhaps most famously, one was said to have crashed at Roswell, New Mexico, in 1947, killing its crew. The bodies, allegedly, ended up in the possession of the federal authorities; when the air force persisted in denying the entire episode, charges of cover-up predictably ensued.

Aliens in Popular Culture

In short order, UFO's and their crews provided the stuff for a cottage industry, engendering sensational books and forming a staple of supermarket tabloids and paperbacks. Among the latter was John G. Fuller's *The Interrupted Journey* (1966), the tale of a New Hampshire couple, Betty and Barney Hill, who claimed to have been abducted by space aliens while driving through the White Mountains. The Hill abduction case established the format for many subsequent narratives whose elements typically included little gray men with huge eyes that wrapped around their heads from front to side and who told their abductees that they were here to help; various invasive, quasi-medical procedures; and the abductees' "recovery" of these and similar memories through hypnosis.

In 1977, the theme of alien abduction crossed over from nonfiction to fiction in Steven Spielberg's immensely successful movie, *Close Encounters of the Third Kind*. This is the tale of a group of humans who singly and severally observe UFO's and develop an obsession with drawing or modeling a mound-like structure. It emerges that space aliens have implanted in them an image of the Devil's Tower, a striking geological formation in Wyoming to which they are meant to travel to attend a public appearance by an alien ship. When the ship duly lands, the aliens disembark a number of U.S. aviators missing since 1945, as well as the child of one of the psychically implanted humans. In appearance, the aliens conform to the little gray (or blue) stereotype, complete with frail bodies and oversized eyes.

Another landmark appeared ten years later in the form of

a nonfiction book entitled *Communion: A True Story*. Its author, a novelist named Whitley Strieber, had been known principally for high-quality thrillers on pacifist and environmentalist themes. Now Strieber claimed to have been mysteriously transported from his upstate New York hideaway into a space ship where he was examined intrusively and then just as mysteriously returned to his bedroom. This proved to be only the first of many encounters with the creatures Strieber called "the visitors," and whom he divided into four separate types. The predominant species would have been familiar to the Hills: about three-and-a-half feet tall, with distended heads, large black oval eyes, rudimentary noses, and thin mouths. The cover art for *Communion* provided what is now the standard iconography of these creatures, including the gray cast of their skin and their jumpsuit-like clothing.

Since *Communion*, Strieber has produced a series of books elaborating upon his ongoing contacts with the visitors—plus his "recovery" that, as a child, he was educated in a secret school near San Antonio, Texas, where he learned to detach his soul from his body and visit such locales as Mars and ancient Rome. He believes that the visitors implant objects of unknown purpose in the bodies of humans, and has detailed his own somewhat ambiguous attempts to remove such an implant from his left ear. The subject of these implants takes up a large part of *Confirmation* (1998), in which Strieber alleges that their existence confirms the truth of the experiences he and others have recounted. . . .

Whether or not Strieber is sane, to him belongs the distinction of having formulated and widely disseminated the standard version of the alien-abduction phenomenon. For nearly a decade, moreover, he occupied the moderate position on the spectrum, the extreme being held down by tabloids enlivened by such matters as the First Lady's plans to adopt a space-alien child. But then, in 1994, the whole debate acquired a certain gravitas with the arrival of Harvard University's John E. Mack.

John Mack's Studies

Abduction, Mack's first book on the subject, was superficially structured like many popular psychiatric works—that is, as a series of case studies. We learn that a number of particularly interesting people had been consulting him professionally since 1990. They were a diverse group—including, among others, a waitress and an immensely successful venture capitalist—but what they had in common was the suspicion or the belief that they had been through exactly the sort of experience reported by Whitley Strieber. Mack customarily hypnotized these people, with the goal of recovering painful memories they might have repressed.

Decent People Can Be Wrong

Psychiatrist John Mack has claimed that his patients [claiming to have been abducted by aliens] have nothing to gain by making up their incredible stories. For some reason it is often thought by intelligent people that only morons are deceived or deluded and that if a person's motives can be trusted then his or her testimony can be trusted, too. While it is true that we are justified in being skeptical of a person's testimony if she has something to gain by the testimony (such as fame or fortune), it is not true that we should trust any testimony given by a person who has nothing to gain by giving the testimony. An incompetent observer, a drunk or drugged observer, a mistaken observer, or a deluded observer should not be trusted, even if he is as pure as the mountain springs once were. The fact that a person is kind and decent and has nothing to gain by lying does not make him or her immune to error in the interpretation of their perceptions.

Robert T. Carroll, *The Skeptic's Dictionary*, 1994–1998.

But here the resemblance to psychiatric case studies ended. For Mack did not treat his subjects; in fact, he did not believe they were in need of treatment, or consider them patients. In his 1999 book, *Passport to the Cosmos*, he refers to them instead as "fellow researchers," and he begins this book by announcing that, since the recollections of his clients did not fit his previous worldview, it came to seem reasonable to him to alter that worldview rather than "continue to force my clients into molds that clearly did not suit them."

There are, Mack tells us, a number of common elements in abduction narratives. Typically, the "experience" begins with bright light, and experiencers see the aliens themselves as "beings of light." They also report powerful and unfamiliar energies: things shake, and experiencers "feel" their bodies, their very cells, vibrating at a higher rate. As for the aliens' "program," or message, this usually has to do with the natural environment—namely, that we on earth are heading for trouble if we do not get serious about curtailing pollution. Sometimes experiencers are shown images of a desolated planet: either a future earth or what the aliens did to their own planet and want us to avoid.

For purposes not entirely clear, the aliens have often collected samples of semen or eggs aboard their ships, and many female experiencers say they have been impregnated with fertilized eggs containing alien genetic material. These impregnations appear to be accomplished by thoroughly clinical means, the fetuses being removed by the aliens during subsequent abductions. Some experiencers report having seen large incubator installations (remarkably similar to those depicted by Aldous Huxley in his dystopian novel, *Brave New World*), while others, evidently having been granted visitation rights, recount ongoing relationships with their hybrid children either aboard ship or in other, unspecified, locations. These sundry activities comprise what Mack calls the Hybrid Project.

In working his way to a set of conclusions from all this reportage, Mack invites us to consider the role of the shaman—the medicine-man figure in primitive cultures who undergoes rigorous training to allow spirit travel into other realities. He discusses the work of three shamans known to him—an American Indian, a Brazilian Indian, and a Zulu (the first of these is a former Green Beret, the second has a Ph.D. in anthropology), the point being to show us that in other cultures, contact with otherworldly beings is routine. "Indigenous people," to use Mack's term, retain knowledge of the "original instructions" of the Creation, and are therefore more in touch with reality than nonindigenous people, who suffer under the burden of the millennia of miseducation otherwise known as civilization.

The "Source"

This brings Mack at last to God—or, to use the term favored by experiencers, to Source—and the big cultural news he wants to tell us. Many of Mack's informants have come to believe that they are not from here, but rather from There. "The ship is my home," one of them says. "I miss my home." Though raised in a rigorously rational and secular Jewish home, Mack himself has arrived at the conviction that we are in a period of spiritual transformation, of which the abduction phenomenon is a powerful engine. Although the aliens (he concedes) are not God, they are nearer to God—to Source—than even the most religious among us; making contact with them, and through them with Source, may thus be the real meaning of the entire phenomenon. He ends by quoting a certain Karin, one of his prize experiencers, as she addresses a meeting of the Friends of the Institute of Noetic Sciences:

> Perhaps it is that we have found ourselves at a fork in the road, and we are once again faced with making a choice. Couldn't we, this time, make the right one? Couldn't we simply reach out and embrace this experience and all that it brings with it, including the terror, as well as the truth, questions and beauty? . . . Please, can't we just this once choose the path that will finally set us free?

Many a psychiatrist, dealing with a patient who claims to have been kidnapped by space aliens and to have had a second personality implanted in his body, might open the diagnostic manual at "S," for schizophrenia. Mack—not for nothing is he a professor of psychiatry at Harvard—is well aware that he must show his experiencers are not crazy. To this end, he diverts us with expositions concerning the workings of his research institute, the testing methods followed by his clinical associates, his screening procedures, and the extent of his erudition as evidenced in multitudinous citations of scholarly sources. Unfortunately, his research procedures evince flaws that even a nontenured alien intruder would recognize.

Mack asserts, first of all, that his own strong suit as a therapist has been the talent for distinguishing the sane from the insane—and that, besides, his experiencers perform well on standardized intelligence and Rorschach tests. Next, he states that as experiencers relate to him their astonishing and sometimes terrifying memories, their "affect" is perfectly appropriate to the narrative: they are deeply emotional, and they evince great physical tension. Moreover, since the story they recount is generally the same, with much circumstantial agreement among individual versions, they must be describing a common reality. Finally, and just to bring things around again, these matters cannot be examined by traditional methods: in the words of the anthropologist Jeremy Narby, quoted approvingly by Mack, "To change what we see, it is sometimes necessary to change what we believe."

Does Sincerity Reveal Truth?

Should we take John Mack's word for it that he knows a madman when he sees one? What if he is himself mad, or perhaps under the influence of an implant? That, at least, might explain the tenacity with which he clings to the notion that emotional affect—"sincerity"—validates the tales told by his experiencers.

In 1692, the adolescent girls of Salem cried out that they had been bewitched by their neighbors; clearly they were possessed by something very important to them, and they manifested all the physical tensions that Mack finds so authenticating. Cotton Mather, the most distinguished American intellectual of his day, was hardly alone in being impressed by the suffering of the "afflicted children" as they confronted their "tormentors" in the courtroom. But no one believes in the spectral persecutions for which the good burghers of Salem went to the gallows.

The Salem "experiencers" are relevant in another regard as well. They all told a remarkably congruent story, leading to the possible conclusion that they, too, were describing a common reality. But the fact is that within days after Betty Parris and Abigail Williams made their first accusations, every teenaged girl in Salem knew what sort of narrative, if told in the courtroom with the right effects, would make her an instant celebrity. It is not necessary to believe that the girls consciously and deliberately fabricated their accounts to understand that the mere fact they told the same story says nothing at all about whether the story was true.

Indeed, considering how long the theme of alien abduction has been available in sources both literary and cinematic, it is odd that a Harvard professor boasting of his analytical acumen should have failed to inquire into the possible non-experiential roots of his clients' narratives. Consider, in this connection, the case of the Zeta Reticulans.

Betty Hill's Map

Betty Hill, the 1961 "abductee" who with her late husband was, so to speak, the patient zero of the phenomenon, reported that one of the aliens aboard ship showed her a star map indicating his home area, and she later made a sketch of it from memory. Several years later, an amateur astronomer named Marjorie Fish applied herself to finding an actual piece of space corresponding with Hill's map. One that satisfied her lay in the vicinity of Zeta Reticuli, a fifth-magnitude double star in the southern constellation known as the Net. Fish's work was taken sufficiently seriously to have generated a 1974 article in the popular journal *Astronomy* averring that her match was very unlikely to occur randomly. Other commentators, including the late Carl Sagan, disagreed rather sharply.

From this beginning, the alien-abduction community has since produced manifold detailed accounts of the lives and loves of the Zeta Reticulans, many of them "channeled" from Zeta Reticuli itself. (A "channel" is a sort of medium who transmits personalities from places and times to which physical travel is not yet available.) A quick search of the Web turns up over 650 hits for the topic, many containing dozens of links to other sites.

What the Zeta Reticuli phenomenon illustrates, in other words, is the immense fertility of minds that truly believe. From a small hint in one abduction narrative there has grown a vast deposit of "fact" about an alleged home planet of the "grays" and about the life they lead there. It is tempting to wonder whether a star with a less allusive name would have been so effective. Snodgrass 242, for example?

But the Hill abduction is the locus of an even more illuminating example of "life" imitating art. The wraparound eyes that are the distinguishing mark of the "grays" first appeared to the world in John G. Fuller's 1966 account of the Hill abduction. It turns out, however, that Betty Hill's notes, written down within days of the event itself, described quite a different alien, with different and less menacing eyes. The wraparound eyes surfaced much later, in a hypnosis session involving her husband on February 22, 1964—as it happens, twelve days after the broadcast of an episode featuring just such wraparound eyes on the science-fiction television show, *The Outer Limits*. It thus seems highly probable that these large and deep orbs, soon to become icons of narrative after narrative of alien abduction, were first created as fiction and only then obligingly if unknowingly confabulated into "reality" by Barney Hill and his hypnotist.

Close Encounters of the Third Kind similarly disseminated an image of little, big-headed, frail-bodied, strange-eyed men, as well as the notion of alien abduction and manipulation of human thought. By the time Whitley Strieber became well-launched into his own series of memoirs, every aspiring abductee with the price of a paperback had the drill down pat. . . .

No Evidence for Abductions

When it comes right down to it, Mack can offer no persuasive evidence against the proposition that his experiencers are either deluded or fraudulent. And if he, a licensed physician, steadfastly refuses to help them shed their delusions or their mendacity, that is because his modal view of them is that they have been through the various extraordinary and improbable experiences they claim, and that alien creatures regularly do visit earth, abduct human beings, impregnate them, harvest their fetuses, and implant foreign objects in their bodies.

It needs to be appreciated that most of these experiencers do not possess fully developed memories of abduction before they come to Mack. Those memories emerge in the course of so-called regressions, or hypnosis sessions, as well as through less dramatic techniques of relaxation. Although Mack maintains that he takes great care not to implant memories where there are none, we have seen how easy it is for some people to conflate memories of different orders of experience, personal and vicarious, not to speak of the vast reservoirs of circumstantial detail ready at hand through the subconscious memory of literary works and movies. No matter how superficially methodical Mack may be, his own status as a believer in the reality of alien abduction cannot but be a potent influence on his clients. In short, he is an enabler.

Passport to the Cosmos is rife with the jargon of New Age "spirituality." Mack has high praise for something called Holotropic Breathwork, a system for inducing "non-ordinary" states of consciousness through controlled breathing and listening to music, and he cites approvingly a quintessentially New Age institution that teaches Brennan Health Science, also known as Hands of Light. There is, one supposes, nothing in principle to stop a New Age physician from taking unhappy people and sending them home with grandiose delusions, especially if they feel less unhappy as a result. Still, one wonders whether the American Psychiatric Association—even in its present, degraded condition—would agree. After all, adopting the rule that the doctor's is the perspective that needs to be altered can lead to putting the lunatics in charge not merely of the asylum but of the psychiatrists, too.

All of which is why, ultimately, John E. Mack of the Harvard Medical School is a much more interesting and distressing phenomenon than any of his poor "fellow researchers." That he, too, shows every outward sign of sincerity is hardly a comfort.

Periodical Bibliography

The following articles have been selected to supplement the diverse views presented in this chapter.

Bob Berman — "Strange Universe," *Astronomy*, March 2001.

Susan Blackmore — "Abduction by Aliens or Sleep Paralysis?" *Skeptical Inquirer*, May/June 1998.

Richard Boylan — "Inside Revelations on the UFO Cover-Up," *NEXUS*, April/May 1998.

Dawn Baumann Brunke — "Alien Probe," *Fate*, June 1999.

Sean Casteel — "The Direction of Our Salvation," *Fate*, September 1998.

John Earls — "Ex-Astronaut Edgar Mitchell Speaks Out on ETs," *Nexus*, December 1998/January 1999.

Cynthia Fox — "The Search for Extraterrestrial Life: Why on Earth Do We Still Believe?" *Life*, March 1, 2000.

Julian Grajewski — "Extraterrestrials Have Never Visited Earth: A Socratic Narrative," *21st Century Science & Technology*, Summer 1998.

Paul Kurtz — "UFO Mythology: The Escape to Oblivion," *Skeptical Inquirer*, July/August 1997.

Susan McClelland and John Betts — "UFOs . . . Seriously: Is There a Middle Ground Between Skepticism and Belief?" *Maclean's*, August 13, 2001.

Gary P. Posner with Philip J. Klass — "ETs May Be Out There . . . But He Says They're Not Here," *Skeptic* (Altadena, CA), Fall 1999.

Kathy Sawyer — "Panel Urges Study of UFO Reports," *Washington Post*, June 28, 1998.

Michael Sturma — "Alien Abductions," *History Today*, January 2000.

Donald E. Tarter — "Looking for God and Space Aliens," *Free Inquiry*, Summer 2000.

Jim Wilson — "Six Unexplainable Encounters: These UFO Sightings Continue to Defy Science and the Skeptics," *Popular Mechanics*, July 1998.

CHAPTER 4

Does Life After Death Exist?

Chapter Preface

With modern advances in medical technology and emergency lifesaving procedures, many people who clinically "die" are resuscitated. Some of those who have gone to the brink of death and lived to tell about it have described strange and remarkable near-death experiences (NDEs). The typical NDE, as depicted by experiencers, involves traveling through a tunnel toward a bright light, feeling warm and peaceful, and encountering deceased loved ones or a religious figure or "being of light" who reassures the experiencer and tells him or her to return to life. Many of those who "come back" believe that they have had a glimpse of the afterlife and feel spiritually transformed by the experience.

In 1975, researcher Raymond Moody wrote *Life After Life*, an influential book that pioneered the field of near-death studies. Moody studied the phenomenon for more than twenty years and became convinced that NDEs prove that life after death exists. "That NDEs totally transform those who experience them demonstrates their reality and power," Moody asserts. Since the publication of *Life After Life*, a growing number of physicians, psychologists, and researchers have seriously examined the NDE phenomenon, drawing conclusions that have led them from their roots in hard science to a field of inquiry that embraces the spiritual. Melvin Morse, for example, is a pediatrician and neuroscientist who has studied NDEs in children for more than fifteen years. Once a die-hard skeptic, Morse now maintains that the NDE is linked to a "God spot" in the brain that allows access to timeless and universal realities.

For those researchers who remain skeptical, however, the NDE offers insight into human physiology and psychology, not the hereafter. Sherwin Nuland, author of *How We Die*, maintains that NDEs are the result of the body's massive release of pain-deadening endorphins, which occurs when one experiences intense physical trauma and fear. Such a release of endorphins—as well as anoxia, a lack of oxygen to the brain—can cause vivid hallucinations. "I think that the mind is just trying to save itself from the horror of unbelievable trauma," contends Nuland. In support of Nuland's theory, several researchers have discovered that many of the characteristics of the NDE can be artificially induced. Neuroscientist Michael A. Persinger has been able to create the sensation of moving through a tunnel to a bright light by stimulating the brain's right temporal lobe with electromagnetic fields. The U.S. Navy has also replicated some features of an NDE—particularly the sense of the presence of a God-like figure—by subjecting test pilots to massive centrifugal forces. "There's nothing magical about the NDE," declares Persinger.

Presently, both skeptics and nonskeptics are drawn to the question of whether NDEs are a window into the beyond or a physiological mechanism that protects the body and the mind during physical trauma. The authors in the following chapter draw on both science and philosophy as they examine the notion of life after death.

"*My explanation to patients [who have had near-death experiences] is that they have glimpsed whatever is on the other side of this physical realm.*"

Near-Death Experiences Are Visions of an Afterlife

James J. Booker III

Many people who come close to dying have vivid near-death experiences (NDEs), writes James J. Booker III in the following viewpoint. Those who have experienced NDEs typically report that they leave their body and are drawn to a bright light that exudes peace and compassion; some people also claim that they encounter dead loved ones and witness a panoramic life review. Booker maintains that the NDE—a psychologically and spiritually transformative event for all who go through it—is a glimpse of life after death. Such experiences should be taken seriously and studied scientifically, he concludes. Booker, a physician, is a member of the International Association for Near-Death Studies.

As you read, consider the following questions:

1. According to Booker, what percentage of people who come close to death have NDEs?
2. What kinds of life changes are reported by those who have experienced NDEs, according to the author?
3. How long have humans been having NDEs, in Booker's opinion?

"Get away from me! Leave me alone, you . . . you . . ."
Mrs. Johnson's sputtering anger took me by surprise. I had, after all, just saved her life.

In her mid-80s, Mrs. Johnson was in the intensive care unit with an acute myocardial infarction. I had been near her room when the cardiac alarm went off, and I arrived with the code blue team. She had gone into ventricular fibrillation and wasn't breathing. The precordial thump had no effect, nor did the initial shock. The second shock, however, converted her to normal sinus rhythm, although she was stuporous and confused.

It was 30 minutes later, when I returned to her room, that Mrs. Johnson lashed out and then refused to speak to me or the nurses. She remained stable, but was still furious when I examined her several hours later. "Why are you so upset when I was successful in bringing you back from death?" I asked.

After a few seconds of silence, she replied, "That's just the point. I didn't want to come back. There I was in a beautiful place, in that wonderful light, and the next thing I know, I'm here in this bed looking up at your ugly face!"

The Near-Death Experience

Now I understood. Mrs. Johnson had had a near-death experience (NDE). NDE is a phenomenon I'm very familiar with, having studied it for more than 30 years. I first became intrigued by NDEs when, as a medical student in 1968, I read a newspaper article about dying people who reported that they had left their bodies and floated. Since then, I've followed the research and joined the International Association for Near-Death Studies. And for 25 years, I've lectured on the topic to college students, church congregations, nursing staffs, retirement communities, teachers, and civic clubs.

But in all that time, I've talked about NDEs with only two doctor groups—during grand rounds at a teaching institution and to a Preferred Provider Organization. For most doctors immersed in objective science, NDEs are too mystical for comfort. And many long-practicing physicians have told me that none of their patients has ever reported an NDE. I'd argue that a handful of their patients probably did have NDEs, but they didn't tell their stories out of fear of being labeled crazy by unsympathetic doctors.

About 15 of my own patients have had NDEs, and many more have described a "nearing death awareness." One of my patients, a man dying of leukemia, was very agitated and frightened. But during rounds one morning, I noticed he was remarkably peaceful. He said a tremendous, bright blue light had briefly appeared in his hospital room the night before and told him not to be afraid. He'd had a nearing death awareness. Other patients described momentary but reassuring visits from a dead child or spouse.

And at nearly every lecture I give, at least one person in the audience says he's had an NDE; often, several people do. A woman who'd had an NDE came to my lecture with her husband, who'd had two! During a talk to a group of people with cardiac defibrillators, nearly half admitted to an NDE. But people generally don't share this profound experience unless they're sure they'll get an empathetic response.

NDE researchers estimate that between 43 and 60 percent of people who come close to death will have a near-death experience. A *US News & World Report* poll found that of the 18 percent of Americans who claimed that they had been on the verge of dying, about one-third, or some 15 million, reported an NDE.

Leaving the Body

So what is an NDE? A woman in extremis hears a loud, unpleasant sound, then finds herself out of her body, floating near the ceiling. She is initially confused at this state of duality, but soon realizes that she has died. She knows where she is and can hear and see, but she can't talk to or touch those she is observing.

She either wills herself toward or is quickly drawn into an open passage. There, she encounters others who telepathically welcome her to this new world, reassuring her that all is well. In the distance is a "being of light," which is brighter than the sun but doesn't hurt her eyes.

As she reaches the light, it conveys an aura of immense knowledge and power, and it bathes her in love, warmth, and compassion. It asks, "Well, how did you do down there?" and she is shown a panorama of her earthly life. The light is nonjudgmental as she and it survey every thought, word, and deed, but she wishes she had done some things differently. They then move into a beautiful landscape, toward a line of trees. As she attempts to pass through, the light says, "You cannot go through to the other side if you want to go back." She replies that this is such a wonderful place she doesn't want to go back. The light says that her life on earth isn't over and she must return.

Stages of the NDE

One of the essential components of the NDE, and certainly the most transformative one, concerns the encounter with the being of light. It is described as similar to being immersed in a sea of unconditional love, which engulfs, soothes, and releases; of being instilled with a feeling of absolute safety, like finding shelter from a storm, or returning to the womb. In fact, the picture painted by experiencers is one of all the archetypes; it is the quintessence of all symbols.

The life review, which brings back not only the most significant events—whether happy or traumatic—but also the ordinary episodes of a person's life, is primarily indicative of the immense power of the human memory, which, for the most part, lies buried in the unconscious. Inaccessible during daily waking life, it is nevertheless present and able to be reactivated during the NDE. This life review—a distressing exercise if ever there was one—takes place in the presence of the being of light, who assists the experiencer in understanding his or her good and bad deeds. Interestingly, the subject experiences at this point whatever emotions, joy, or pain his or her words or acts may have produced in others. The experiencer's remorse and guilt feelings are eased by the kindness of the being of light, who points out mistakes in order to help him or her improve, not to punish. This stage of the NDE is once again highly symbolic, for it is linked to the notion of good and evil—one of the fundamental archetypes. In this context, and from the purely logical standpoint, it is difficult to see the usefulness of such an exercise, unless from the perspective of a future in which these lessons may be applied.

Evelyn Elsaesser Valarino, *On the Other Side of Life*, 1997.

Suddenly she finds herself back in her earthly body. Like Mrs. Johnson, she's angry about being back, but eventually she accepts her return as something that was meant to be.

She realizes she has further work to do here before going to that other realm.

The length of an NDE varies; it can be as "complete" as the one described above, or it might entail just an over-whelming sense of peace and love, the bright light, or the out-of-body experience. Not all NDEs are pleasant, however. People who are self-destructing through alcohol or drugs may report seeing their life as a void, and highly controlled individuals may be terrified by the out-of-body experience, especially zipping into the open passage.

A Transformative Event

Regardless of its quality and content, an NDE transforms people forever. They gain a greater purpose in life, they feel they should love others unconditionally, and they quest after knowledge of how the world works. Some acquire psychic ability, which can be very unsettling. One patient told me she'd had an NDE as a teenager, and since then has been able to predict events. After she foretold three of her relatives' deaths, her family treated her as a pariah, thinking that she had somehow influenced their dying.

Those who have an NDE may have difficulty readjusting to earthly time and three-dimensional space. Conflicts with spouses or family are common, occasionally leading to estrangement and divorce. The wife of a man who had "returned" told me she wanted her curmudgeonly husband back; she couldn't cope with his post-NDE sweetness and gentleness. Another problem is that the body's electromagnetic field can be changed after an NDE, so the person's quartz watch no longer keeps time.

Skeptics offer all sorts of explanations for the NDE phenomenon—anoxia, high carbon dioxide levels, endorphin release, even wish fulfillment and a desire to relive the birth process. Sure, physical events like anoxia can trigger an NDE, but they can't account for the psychological transformation that results or the similarity of so many people's experiences. My explanation to patients is that they have glimpsed whatever is on the other side of this physical realm.

The near-death experience seems to be as old as mankind, rather than a recent manifestation of our ability to more easily resuscitate those in extremis. Archaeologists have found Neanderthal man buried with clothing and implements, as if outfitted for travel to another world. This concept of an afterlife most likely came from NDEs. Writings in *The Tibetan Book of the Dead* clearly indicate that the ancient Tibetan monks were familiar with NDEs, and Plato's warrior, Er, describes his experience on the funeral pyre in terms that could have come straight out of today's NDE literature.

Because of the powerful aftermath of an NDE, physicians need to become familiar with the phenomenon. It's important to listen to NDE descriptions with acceptance and compassion, and to reassure patients who have "come back" that they're not crazy. I tell patients that NDEs are known occurrences, and their feelings are normal and will eventually become less intense.

The Value of NDEs

Doubters will say, "But NDEs are not real. Why give credence to something that is illusory?" I like to paraphrase the philosopher William James, who said that spiritually moving experiences, which are solely personal, have intrinsic value if they have meaning for the individual. Therefore, it's counterproductive for physicians to attempt to "set the record straight." Physicians who are not comfortable discussing NDEs should refer patients to those who are. The International Association for Near-Death Studies is a good source for finding support groups.

Learning about NDEs not only has helped me counsel those who have gone through them, but it's allowed me to give patients close to death or frightened of death a more substantial concept of an afterlife than is accorded by faith alone.

The NDE is an integral part of human existence, and it should be scientifically studied to support the ancient physician's oath: "I will follow the method of treatment that, according to my ability and judgment, I consider for the benefit of my patients."

> "The near-death experience . . . is the
> mind's attempt to preserve the 'self'
> against the looming reality of death."

Near-Death Experiences May
Not Be Visions of an Afterlife

Harvard Health Letter

In the following viewpoint, the editors of the *Harvard Health Letter* maintain that there could be mundane explanations for so-called near-death experiences (NDEs)—occurrences in which people who have nearly died claim to have left their bodies and caught glimpses of an afterlife. Some researchers contend that the brain of a dying person may undergo an episode of dissociation, a form of psychological escape that can occur in response to trauma or stress. Other scientists argue that NDEs could result from the body's release of euphoria-inducing chemicals or from a lack of oxygen to the brain, both of which could lead to temporal lobe seizures that produce hallucinations. The *Harvard Health Letter* is a monthly newsletter published by the Harvard Medical School.

As you read, consider the following questions:

1. Who first described the near-death experience in a clinical way, according to the writers of this viewpoint?
2. According to researchers cited by the authors, what is the possible evolutionary explanation for near-death experiences?
3. What are some of the negative effects of near-death experiences, according to the authors?

Obviously, what we know about near-death experiences comes from survivors. Raymond Moody coined the term near-death experience in *Life After Life*, his 1975 book about 100 people who nearly died. The near-death experience was first described in a clinical way in 1892 by Albert von St. Gallen Heim, a Swiss geology professor. Prompted by his own nearly fatal fall in a mountain climbing accident, Heim published a collection about the mental experiences of other people who had fallen, been wounded in war, or nearly drowned.

The content of the near-death experience varies by culture and expectations about death. Some of the most common elements, however, include a sense of peace, out-of-body experiences in which the people believe they can see themselves being rescued or resuscitated, perceptions of entering a tunnel with a bright light at the end, and panoramic life review. Some commentators have noted that the tunnel image and life review are more common among people in the West than in other parts of the world.

Psychological Explanations

The standard psychological explanation for the near-death experience is that it is the mind's attempt to preserve the "self" against the looming reality of death. It has features of what psychiatrists call depersonalization, a sense of detachment or estrangement. Some have suggested that the out-of-body experience is an extreme extension of the detachment aspects of depersonalization. Yet in other situations, depersonalization is often unpleasant and brings on anxiety, panic, and a feeling of emptiness. Some believe that the near-death experience more closely resembles an episode of dissociation, a psychological state when strong and usually unpleasant emotions get separated from ideas or situations so that the person can delay experiencing the emotions—or avoid them altogether. Daydreaming is a mild, often enjoyable form of dissociation. But dissociation is also used to describe the psychological escape experienced by trauma and rape victims. Bruce Greyson, a University of Virginia researcher who has written extensively about near-death experiences, published a study in the Feb. 5, 2000, *Lancet*, of 96 people who had had near-death experiences and, for comparison, 38 who had not. Based on questionnaires designed to tease out dissociative symptoms, Greyson concluded that dissociation as a response to stress is the most plausible psychological explanation for the near-death experience.

Explanations for NDEs

Physiological findings have led many researchers to view NDEs not as glimpses into a world beyond but as insights into the world within the human mind. "I think it is an evolutionary adaptation," says Sherwin Nuland, the National Book Award–winning author of *How We Die*. He ascribes NDEs to the actions of opiate-like compounds known as endorphins, which are released by the brain at times of great physical stress to deaden pain and alleviate fear. He scoffs at those who view NDEs as a temporary bridge to an afterlife. "I think that the mind is just trying to save itself from the horror of unbelievable trauma," he says.

Daniel Alkon, chief of the Neural Systems Laboratory at the National Institutes of Health, says anoxia (oxygen deprivation in the brain) lies at the root of all NDEs. When death appears certain, he argues, the body will often shut down and "play dead" as a last course of action. His skepticism is significant because many years ago, as a result of a hemorrhage, he had a near-death experience himself.

Brendan Koerner, *U.S. News & World Report*, March 31, 1997.

Some have suggested that rather than being an escape from reality, the near-death experience is actually based on the realistic sense of relief that the pain and suffering of dying is over. It has also been suggested that the near-death experience may be the mind's way of conserving energy reserves. Still others see an altruistic streak to the near-death experience: it has survived through the thousands of years of evolution because it makes death less frightening to others.

Physiological Explanations

Near-death experiences also can be explained at the physiological level. One possibility is that the stress of dying triggers a massive release of endorphins, the brain chemicals that kill pain and produce euphoria. Some have pointed out that these experiences might simply be a consequence of a brain starved for oxygen. Endorphins or lack of oxygen may also set off seizures, abnormal firings of brain cells, in the temporal lobe, the part of the brain that plays an important role in memory and hearing. Similarly, abnormal firings of brain cells in the visual cortex, the part of the brain that processes sight, might explain the tunnel and bright lights element of near-death experiences. Because the visual cortex is organized so that many cells are devoted to the center of the visual field and relatively few to the periphery, abnormal firings of the visual cortex brain cells could create a tunnel effect and the sensation of seeing a bright light.

When people survive brushes with death, the near-death mental state tends to have a positive effect. Generally, people have a greater appreciation for life, don't dwell on death as much, and have more concern for others. People tend to become more spiritual after near-death experiences. This is true even for people who have attempted suicide. Some studies have shown that near-death experiences among suicide attempters tend to reduce future attempts.

There are important exceptions to the positive effects. People who go through a near-death experience can come to doubt their sanity. Or, the near-death experience can be deeply upsetting because it doesn't jibe with the person's religious beliefs. Some people get depressed and angry about being "returned" from what they perceive as a happier afterlife. Moreover, some researchers have argued that all the attention paid to the blissful near-death experience has led to neglect of the hellish experience that some go through. The idea of a deeply satisfying end to life is attractive. But perhaps as the poet Dylan Thomas would have it, many of us do not go gentle into that good night.

"The concept of past lives, or reincarnation, has played an important role throughout history."

Past-Life Therapy Offers Proof of Reincarnation

Martin Patton

Martin Patton is president of the International Medical and Dental Hypnotherapy Association and a Certified Past Life Trainer. In the following viewpoint, Patton discusses how his work as a hypnotherapist revealed to him that humans experience multiple physical lifetimes. Clients who came to him for treatment of anxiety and phobias would often regress to a past lifetime under hypnosis, he maintains. Eventually Patton learned the method of past-life therapy, which incorporates guided hypnosis to help clients recall events in former lives and how they may be influencing the individual's present life. Patton notes that reincarnation, a central tenet of several eastern religions, has been embraced by such notable westerners as Benjamin Franklin.

As you read, consider the following questions:
1. How does past-life therapy bring about spiritual healing, in Patton's opinion?
2. What did Patton's female client discover about her anger when she underwent past-life regression?
3. What is the *Tibetan Book of the Dead* devoted to, according to the author?

From "Reincarnation . . . " by Martin Patton, *Subconsciously Speaking*, July 2001. Copyright © 2001 by Infinity Institute International, Inc. Reprinted with permission.

W hat hogwash! Why would anyone want to know if they have lived before?

Sound familiar? Maybe one of you has said this in the past. Heaven knows I did! The first five past life regressions I did were mostly by accident and I didn't believe. I had asked the clients to go back to the cause of the problem and found them in past lives. Scared the daylights out of me when they described themselves back in another time. But we worked it through and they got better that day. Wow, a therapy that worked successfully right away. I continued to see people with phobias and anxieties who were immediately relieved of their problem. My unbelief continued for perhaps the next 100 clients. I thought they were making it up and were justifying their illness with a story they saw in a movie or read in a book. Then I encountered a four-year-old who couldn't possibly be making it up and a seventeen-year-old male who took me back to six lifetimes, four of which were as females. The realism and factual information from these two in particular changed my mind. The next 5,550-plus cases more than convinced me that this is a viable and needed therapy.

In the beginning I knew I needed to learn more, and I studied with Irene Hickman and Bill Baldwin in meetings arranged in Detroit. I heard Bill and Dick Sutphen speak at the 1987 American Board of Hypnotherapy conference in Orange County, California and was impressed with their knowledge and abilities. I learned Past Lives and Spirit Releasement from Bill and assisted him in a number of classes, including those he taught at Irene's house in Kirksville, Missouri. Learning Past Life Regression and Past Life Therapy changed my life more than anyone will ever know.

Past Life Regression

Past Life Regressing is the experience of going back in time, reexperiencing a previous lifetime. Some folks do this for the personal knowledge of how and why these past life events are affecting their present lifetimes. They do it to get a handle on why things are happening and what they can do to make them better. In other words, they are curious and want to know who and what they were before, and what they need to do to take advantage of that knowledge in this lifetime.

Past Life Therapy is used for emotional and spiritual healing. The emotions of the past are sometimes carried into the present with the same souls. Interaction of the souls in this life may more easily be explained if you know the situations of the past life that created them. More often than not, the people who you are living with in this lifetime were also in past lifetimes. As the client reviews these emotional responses in the past, it gives that client the ability to understand the emotional responses of the present.

Spiritual healing results in the knowing of your purpose in this lifetime and what decisions you made in the past that are affecting your lifetime today. Many times the reason other people are in our lives today is directly related to experiences from the past. Once understanding of this life is accomplished, changes can take place that allow for spectacular growth. We are blocked spiritually from moving forward in this lifetime if we are ignorant of why we are here and what it is we are doing in this life.

One Woman's Past Life

A lady came to me, recommended by a good friend. She was angry all of the time and on a second marriage that was falling apart. She was angry with others around her—neighbors, her kids' teachers, herself, and anyone else with whom she came in contact. She was very unlikable. When we went back into her past, she was a French girl of about 13. Her parents were Jewish and France had just been overrun by the Nazis. She was arrested, along with a whole bunch of Jewish children, and was being sent to a concentration camp by way of a railway boxcar. Since she was a little older, she was placed in charge of the younger children in the car. The boxcar also contained adults. As they were being moved, the boxcar developed a defective wheel and had to be pushed off onto a siding and was abandoned and locked. Without food or water, they began to die. They called out to the townspeople near the siding and could see them through the slats of the car and knew they were being heard. But no one came to help. Some of the others would eat those who had died, and they all eventually starved and died. She was angry with those religious people in the boxcar who did not respect the dying; angry at those in the town who did nothing; angry at the authority figures who let them die. This woman kept the anger, died and came back into this lifetime angry.

Christianity and Reincarnation

Christianity did not have a problem with reincarnation until the third century A.D. It was then that Emperor Justinian convened his Second Council at Constantinople as a reaction to the teachings of Origen, the Church Father most associated with the doctrine of reincarnation. Origen's reputation as a learned and devout Christian puts him on par with St. Thomas Aquinas. St. Augustine went so far as to call him "the most learned man in Christian history," and the *Encyclopaedia Britannica* says that he was "the most prominent and prolific of all the Church Fathers"—so his opinions should not be lightly dismissed. With this in mind, Origen's famous statement on transmigration can be quoted:

"By some inclination toward evil, certain souls come into bodies, first of men; then, due to association with the irrational passions after the allotted span of human life, they are changed into beasts, from which they sink to the level of plants. From this condition they rise again through the same stages and [are] restored to their heavenly place."

Steven J. Rosen, *Fate*, May 1998.

Then we started to review that lifetime of the angry 13-year-old and the people she saw in this life as teachers, religious people, authority figures and neighbors. Spiritually she had brought back with her three of the children who had died under her care. After we released these entities, she saw that she was living with people who were in that lifetime with her. Her first husband was one of the guards that left the boxcar on the siding, two of her children were under her care on the train, and her present husband was one of the townspeople who failed to assist. She realized that she was working out the trauma of that death; her second husband was trying to make up for his lack of courage in that previous lifetime; and her children chose her to protect them in this lifetime. Her anger subsided. She changed immediately, so much so that she was elected to head a children's Christmas charity. She became a strong Christian lady who loved her neighbors. And, most importantly, she was no longer angry.

Knowledge of past lives can shed light on your talents, preferences, aversions and strengths, sometimes in surprising ways. The lady above was naturally fluent in French and majored in French in college. If you are a talented musician, chances are you developed your skill over many lifetimes of training and practice. Occasionally people discover talents they didn't know they had until they delve into their past lives. With a moderate amount of training to refresh your memory and tune up your present-life body, it may be possible to revive long dormant skills. Most likely your strongest friendships today began long before you were born—this time.

Reincarnation

The concept of past lives, or reincarnation, has played an important role throughout history. Belief in multiple physical lifetimes is included in several religious doctrines, including the Bible. The ancient scripture included in the *Tibetan Book of the Dead* is devoted to helping a person end one life and cross over to the next. In many eastern religions, the idea of Karma, or in more colloquial terms, what goes around comes around, is the golden rule that keeps behavior in line, cautioning that even if you get away with wrongdoing in this life, you will be held accountable in the next.

Reincarnation was the generally accepted philosophy prior to Christianity, where reincarnation was replaced for some with the belief that Christ has atoned for our sins and we can go straight to Heaven without having to bear multiple lifetimes. Regardless of the popularity of Christian thought, notable statesman and author Benjamin Franklin had a keen interest in reincarnation.

The concept of coming back experienced a western revival during the twentieth century. Edgar Cayce, founder of ARE, the Association for Research and Enlightenment, claims to have remembered many lives in a trance state. Many consider Cayce a modern day prophet and his written work extensively covers the subject of rebirth.

Many hypnotherapists incorporate past life regression hypnosis and therapy to help people understand their present challenges by resolving issues further back than childhood. This therapy usually consists of guided hypnosis to regress back to former lifetimes. Most remember unspectacular lifetimes similar to the lifetime they are living now. One woman reviewed with me a rather placid life in the past, very ordinary and common. When we were reviewing that life, she got very upset and stated that she was doing the same thing over again in this lifetime. In this life she should be writing and she was taking the easy way again. She raised her children and started writing, and today she is a bestselling author.

An important concept when considering past lives is the concept of soul mates, two spirits that will interact in some fashion life after life. This concept has been used to explain premature intimacy based on that feeling that you have known a virtual stranger forever.

Doubt does occur because, although there are many documented cases, most people do not consciously remember a past life. Some believe that the memory is wiped clean by the trauma of rebirth and that carrying our past lives around like baggage from life to life would be too burdensome and traumatizing for the average person. In my experience, the recall of past lives has only helped in overcoming this life's problems. Sometimes the memories are triggered by a dream that becomes very real; other times by coincidence. A friend was walking across the battlefield at Gettysburg, tripped, and remembered being there and being shot on that spot. Others have visited cities and known instinctively what was around the corner. Remembering past lives is not just for the most enlightened; all seem to benefit from the experience.

"Like it or not, things end. Personally I work better under a deadline."

Reincarnation Does Not Exist

Kat Meltzer

In the following viewpoint, Kat Meltzer explains why she rejects the notion that people live multiple lifetimes. For one thing, she points out, the only proof in support of reincarnation comes from accounts from the dead, who are supposedly "channeled" to the living through a psychic or medium. Such "statements" from the dead, however, are either ridiculous or trite—obviously concocted by the so-called mediums. The idea of reincarnation, moreover, undermines any motivation for social or personal responsibility, since it encourages people to believe that their life choices are largely determined by fate. Ultimately, Meltzer concludes, belief in reincarnation leads to a callous indifference about the value of life. Meltzer is a freelance writer based in San Francisco.

As you read, consider the following questions:
1. What did the author do to test the reliability of channeling?
2. Why would extinction not be a problem if reincarnation were the way of the universe, in Meltzer's opinion?
3. Why does Meltzer object to the notion that people choose the circumstances of their own birth?

From "Change the Channel," by Kat Meltzer, *Skeptical Inquirer*, July/August 1998. Copyright © 1998 by The Committee for the Scientific Investigation of Claims of the Paranormal. Reprinted with permission.

R eincarnation: brought to you by the same earnest folk who remind you to "Be here now."

Still it's satisfying to think that the yutz who didn't want to miss his exit so he cut across three lanes without signalling, missed you by a foot, drove up the embankment to the road, then flipped you the bird, may one day return as a lowly slug and get eaten by a scrub jay.

And who couldn't use a second chance? A friend once told me "When I come back, I'm going to be a dolphin. I want to be sleek and have a blowhole." Well, yes. Who wouldn't?

Channeling

So how do we know we get do-overs? What proof do we have that the cosmos dishes out gold stars and frownie faces? The channeled statements of the dead. If this is the case, I wouldn't be in such a hurry to advertise. Death, it seems, is not very good for you.

First of all, dead people get seriously stupid. Dumber than a chunk of sidewalk. Einstein, who believed mathematics was poetry, the language of the universe, could no longer calculate a square root. I once asked a channeler to contact Murray Gell-Mann. I realize the esteemed Dr. Gell-Mann, may his big brain scintillate for decades to come, is not dead. [Gell-Mann is the Nobel Prize–winning physicist who discovered the quark, a subatomic particle.] I just wanted to see what would happen. Forgive me, I had no idea quarks were a gift from an ancient Pleidian named Izzy-Ra. Also, I don't want to alarm you, but I tried your kugel recipe. I grovel before your superior talents, sir, but I think I'll go back to boiling the noodles before baking.

Don't take my word for it. Ask a dead person a question. Nothing tricky, like "What's the Hubble constant?" or "Why is 'phonetics' not spelled phonetically?" Ask him or her something easy. Ask the person where I lost my keys. Then call me. If I find them, it's one point for the born-again-and-agains.

You also have to wonder about their seductive maunderings. "It's beautiful here, it's so peaceful, your puppy who got run over when you were five is waiting for you!" Doesn't this sound just the smallest bit like a telemarketer? What if the dead are actually working a pyramid con scheme? What if channelers and mediums are actually focus group facilitators? What if all those beckoning figures at the end of the tunnel are there to get you to sign something?

And what if, behind that bright loving light, are the dead, wearing headsets and punching autodialers? And the biggest, shiniest guy of all floats around their drab cubicles barking [motivational speeches]?

No Motivation to Repent

Or maybe existence on the other side of the veil really is all chirpy and cheery and pink and gooshy. This is not good news for me. I would not cope well with this afterlife. I can't stand perky people on this side. I want to bite them but I'm afraid they'll stick to my teeth. Promise me, I beg you, if I return to spout trite insights, you will dig me up, scoop out my heart with a rusty spoon and boil it in balsamic vinegar.

Which brings up another problem. How come the dead don't whine? So what if everything's so beautiful and perfect on the other side? Everybody whines! What the hell happens to these dead people?

Remember your Auntie Crab and Uncle Burp, who found fault with everything. Eventually Auntie Crab crumps. At the funeral everyone finally exhales. Then they take turns imitating her griping about the eulogy, the turnout, little black dresses, cheap hooch, and Jell-O salad. Six months later Auntie Crab starts sending messages. Now that she's dead, she is finally truly happy. The implication here is that the best thing we can do for the chronic kvetch in our life is put her down, like an evil incontinent cat.

Speaking of which, how come we never hear from anyone in hell? For motivation to repent, it would be hard to beat a voice from the fiery pit. I can only imagine:

Me: Uncle Burp? Is that you?

Medium: AAARRRGGGHHH!

Then there are the apocalyptic predictions. Nothing like a touch of death to inspire grandiosity. The Skinner box part of life eludes some guy through his entire pre-moribund existence. He expires operantly unconditioned. Now he's back and he's really chatty about the impending doom of humanity. Lots of finger-shaking from beyond the grave. This from a man who died in a tragic anvil experiment—after all, the coyote always walked away. [Developed by behavioral psychologist B.F. Skinner, a Skinner-box contains one or more levers that an animal can press to obtain a reward. Operant conditioning occurs when the animal learns to press a lever to receive food.]

WHY EVERYONE WAS ALWAYS SOMEBODY IN THEIR PREVIOUS LIFE.

Pudim. © 1993 by *Skeptical Inquirer*. Reprinted with permission.

Maybe, just maybe, this time the species is on the verge of extinction. Humans are special, and I'm fond of several of them. I do not want to become extinct. But suppose it happens. Suppose we poison, fry, and detonate our species to oblivion. Homo sapiens circles the drain and is sucked at last beyond the Great U-Bend. What happens? We come back as sulfur-loving microbes clustered at scalding breaches in the sea floor under countless tons of water, and we work our way up to being cockroaches. And we deserve it for being so careless as to lay waste to an entire planet.

If reincarnation is the way of the cosmos, then extinction should not be a problem. Time is on the side of Life with a capital L. If it doesn't include a certain bunch of great apes, the ones who shave, the ones who diet, the universe will go right on expanding. Presumably Life will find a way to carry on.

Reincarnation offers a placebo for thanatophobia, and placebos can be amazingly effective. Why get all prickly about such a cuddly, hopeful belief? Well, if you calculate the ratio of bodies to souls, you have to bring in vast numbers of souls from other planets to make the math work out. It perverts personal responsibility to a control freak's dream: You choose the circumstances of your birth. It also replaces social responsibility with fate.

Grades After Death?

Because it replaces social responsibility with fate. You bumble through life, you die, you get your grades. (Think of it. You're going to hear "Not living up to your potential" even when you're dead.) You are assigned to your next life as a punishment or as a reward. Good news, perhaps, for babies Donald Trump and Bill Gates. Hurrah for the divine right of kings! But consider a starving Tutsi toddler who watched his room get hacked to pieces by the neighbors. What do you say? "Let's get you the hell out of here and by the way, have a sandwich." Or "Firm but fair, laddie. You musta really screwed up last time. I sure hope you learned your lesson."

Because it perverts personal responsibility to a control freak's dream. In this version, you, not Mrs. Grundy or the archetypal Dad, choose the circumstances of your birth. The essentials come from Tibetan Buddhism, a wise and compassionate tradition. Remember all the stoners who read *The Tibetan Book of the Dead* [a Tibetan Buddhist guide for the dead and dying]? Maybe it was the dope, maybe it was television, but we now have a population with the attention span of a chihuahua. A very American Chihuahua full of pioneer spirit, can-do enthusiasm, and a nasty little territorial domain habit. An American Chihuahua for the millennium who barks the Twelve-Step slogan: "Take what you like and leave the rest."

We'll take the "choice of rebirth" part. Choices put us in the driver's seat. And thirty-one flavors and 500 channels aren't enough. So why did I choose myopia, chubby knees, and a predisposition to heart disease? Never mind, I'm sure I had my reasons. We'll even take the Bardo concept [the Tibetan Buddhist belief in an "in-between place," the state in which one thing ends and another begins]—sort of a postmortem Department of Motor Vehicles, right? Purgatory with a lot of waiting in line?

But the lifetime of meditation, service, and discipline required to calm the mind so that the soul can withstand the onslaught of forty-two peaceful deities, fifty-eight wrathful ones, flashing lights, the whirlwinds of karma, a barrage of visions—excuse me, my beeper just went off. What was I saying? Oh yeah, the vision thing. Who has the time?

Think of weary cafeteria ladies, janitors who sign their paychecks with an X, junkie babies, schizophrenics who sleep in cardboard boxes. A psychic once told me my profoundly retarded sister had chosen her brain and body so that she could help my mother grow. I asked if he could see any dental work in his future. He didn't get it.

Accepting the concept of reincarnation leads to a callousness about life and a callowness about death. Because when we invoke the power of choice where there is no power and no choice, we pass the irretrievable minutes of the one life we are sure of in illusion. And real choices, hard ones, are waiting.

Like it or not, things end. Personally I work better under a deadline.

"The traditional concept of life after death has died."

Eternal Life as Traditionally Conceived Does Not Exist

John S. Spong

In the following viewpoint, John S. Spong takes issue with the traditional Christian concept of life after death. Spong contends that the early institutional church developed the notion of heaven and hell as a means to control human behavior and enforce conformity. After the nineteenth century, however, the idea of a God who metes out eternal reward or punishment for human actions was challenged by psychological and sociological insights into human motivation. Moreover, the conventional understanding of heaven and hell came to be seen as self-centered, as it assumes that good behavior is motivated by a selfish desire for a reward rather than for the sake of goodness itself. Heaven is a transcendent state of being in which one is selflessly open to God, the author maintains, not a place of future reward. Spong is a retired bishop of the Episcopal diocese of Newark, New Jersey.

As you read, consider the following questions:
1. What are the four dilemmas that undermined the believability of the church's understanding of life after death, according to Spong?
2. In the author's opinion, how did the loss of belief in an afterlife help give birth to liberal politics?
3. What is God, in Spong's view?

Thesis #11: "The hope of life after death must be separated forever from the behavior control mentality of reward and punishment. The Church must abandon, therefore, its reliance on guilt as a motivator of behavior."

—From the twelve theses drawn from the book
Why Christianity Must Change or Die

"If a person dies, shall he/she live again?" For a significant number of people this question, framed by Job, is the most important question that is addressed by their religious convictions. The ability to determine a person's ultimate destiny has been the source of the greatest power that religious bodies have amassed. Wherever that institutional power has been exercised in the social order, the primary result has been to enforce human conformity to cultural standards and to control behavior. The enforcing lever has been the claim that the religious institution spoke for God who had the divine ability to reward or to punish. So effectively has this power been exercised by the Christian Church throughout its history, that guilt came to be associated with the Church as the emotion most often elicited. It was not enough for the Church to promise earthly blessing for a life well lived, for evil too often seemed to be rewarded and goodness punished. Given the presuppositions out of which our ancestors operated, it became a theological necessity to provide both a heavenly realm [and a place] where eternal flames would engulf those whose actions were contrary to the Church's stated values, but in our day, this reservoir of enormous ecclesiastical power has dissipated and little conviction exists today about life after death.

There are, I believe, at least four serious problems that have coalesced to destroy the believability of most of the Church's understanding of life after death. They have to be lifted into our consciousness and examined if we are to be believers once again.

Questioning Traditional Views

First, the traditional view of life after death was predicated on a theistic understanding of God. The God who dispensed heaven and hell was an external, supernatural parent figure who, to listen to the preachers from this era, spent all of the divine time keeping record books on everything anyone did that would form the basis of final judgment. So pervasive was this concept that jokes about particular confrontations with St. Peter at the "pearly gates" became a recognizable part of our western humor. But as our view of the universe expanded from Copernicus and Galileo to space travel the idea of a record-keeping theistic deity somewhere just above the sky became less and less believable. [When] God [as] understood in these theistic categories faded, so also did those parts of our theological system directly dependent on that god definition. Conviction about life after death was a major casualty.

The second problem developed with the rise of a sociological consciousness in the 19th century, when the medieval patterns built on class distinctions and racial differences in the human family were seriously challenged by a rising sense of democracy that took centuries to develop fully. First, the divine right of kings, the linchpin of this social stability, was compromised by the adoption of the Magna Carta [the charter of English civil and political liberties signed by King John in 1215]. Next, innate ability rather than god-given status began to be valued. Finally, we began to look at the radical inequality found in the variety of starting places in life and to see how unfair the sense judgment we had once attributed to God really was. Novelists like Charles Dickens and Victor Hugo posed these issues for us in dramatic ways. Is the poor child, abused by society because of his poverty, to be judged by God on the same basis as one born to privilege? Is stealing a loaf of bread, when that is the only way one's family might escape starvation, to be judged on the same basis as one who stole as a way of life? Shortly after the theistic deity who kept record books on individual deeds began to fade, the basis upon which that theistic deity made divine judgments and dispensed reward or punishment began to be questioned and destabilized.

An Unfair Heaven?

The third problem gnawing at this once powerful religious conviction came in the psychological revolution that arrived in the first half of the 20th century, bringing the collapse of that naive individualism upon which the judgment of this theistic deity was presumably based. If a psychologically abused child grows up to be a murdering adult, where does blame lie? Can an individual deed be judged on its own merits or must we be aware of the extenuating circumstances shaping that person's life? If we do that, how do we assess blame sufficiently to enable divine reward or punishment to be dispensed appropriately? Suddenly heaven began to seem unfair and hell unjust, no matter what we believed about the record-keeping theistic deity.

God's Being

The church seems to almost assume that God can be contained in her sacraments, her scriptures, her rites, and theology. We would never say this, but by habit we act as if God is confined to the cult of the church, as if conventional congregational life says it all about God! But God is far greater, wilder, and freer than all this. Our religion is only a small expression of the Creator, for God's being is expressed in infinite form. God will not be limited by our piety or owned by whatever forms we develop, however good or useful they may be. To recognize this is to begin to see God everywhere, to release God's divine reality from its imaginary religious prison, so that God charges everything with life, direction, and love.

Brian C. Taylor, *Setting the Gospel Free*, 1996.

The fourth reason brings, in my opinion, the profoundest challenge of all. That objection comes when we recognize the radical self-centeredness of the motivation that such a belief creates. The reason for goodness is not that goodness is itself a virtue, but rather to enable one to achieve rewards or avoid punishments. This viewpoint assumes that goodness cannot be motivated on its own merits, but must be encouraged by the selfish desires of reward or the fear of being punished. Heaven and hell therefore are vestiges of this radical self-centeredness.

So under pressure from each of these four serious compromising objections, the concept of life after death has entered a theological limbo. The Church will not abandon it officially; but few theologians seek to engage this profound issue, because it makes little sense inside the box of traditional theistic thinking and no one has proposed a new context in which it can be examined. So in both conservative and liberal Christian circles, a conspiracy of silence has fallen on the subject. In a 1997 *Time* cover story the issue life after death was said to be ignored across the Christian spectrum. It has become nothing more than pious rhetoric employed frequently in the home of the deceased. The word "heaven" has been transformed into an adjective and applied to an ice cream flavor known as "heavenly hash," or it is used in romantic language to describe what it is like to be with one's beloved. The word "hell" has become a mild oath, which has clearly lost most of its traditional content when one can say "It's cold as hell today."

The Passion for Justice

Historians suggest that this loss of confidence in an afterlife created the passion that gave birth to liberal politics. Both communism and socialism in Europe, as well as the emergence of those programs called the New Deal, the Great Society and the War on Poverty in the United States have been expressions of this phenomenon. A passion to address the injustices of human life lay dormant in western civilization as long as the conviction held that these injustices would be addressed in an afterlife. When the power of that conviction began to fade, human beings, seeing this world as their only time to live, were no longer willing to be passive. So the driving passion for racial and ethnic equality, gender fairness and the end of homophobic prejudices became major 20th century issues. The poor no longer viewed their status as the will of god, and so agitation to improve their status emerged with vigorous force. None of this occurred until the anticipation of life after death retreated from the consciousness of our modern world.

Right wing conservative voices will immediately deny these insights. They do not want to face the fact that the traditional concept of life after death has died and a vacuum exists in the very place where their religious power once resided. That is why Thesis #11 raises such anger among them and why no significant conservative voice is wrestling publicly with this issue.

Life after death, understood as a place of reward and punishment, must, I now believe, be jettisoned from the Christianity that hopes to live into the third millennium. It has died already. A slight breeze blowing in its direction will topple it publicly. The days when guilt can be used by the Church as a weapon of behavior control are over.

The Ground of Being

But having said that let me now state my deep conviction that our conscious life is not ended with our biological death. For me this is a certainty that arises out of the heart of the gospel, but I could not see it until I escaped the boundaries of theism which has captured that Gospel for most of its two thousand years. For me, God is no longer a supernatural being eternal to life. God is rather the very ground and source of Being itself. This means that the more deeply I live and love and have the courage to be the self I am, the more fully God can be seen and revealed in my being.

Jesus is not for me the incarnation of a distant theistic deity, but he remains the ultimate revelation of God for me because his humanity was so complete he became the perfect conduit through which the reality of God as Being itself could be seen, engaged and experienced. When I "live and move and have my being in God," as Paul suggested, I enter that presence which transcends my every limit including my mortality. When I am able to be an agent of life to another, I discover as a grace-filled serendipity that the words of Francis of Assisi are correct, that it is in giving that I receive, in loving that I am loved and in dying that I am raised to new life. So heaven for me is not a place of reward. It is the experience of the fullness of Being. Hell is not a place of punishment. It is the experience of non-Being. I can taste both of these realities now in those relationships that call me beyond my fears and prejudices and in those relationships which shred my personhood. I grow not by seeking to be good, but by experiencing that love that sets me to be, and acting on that love, as a giver of what I have received, and as an agent of another's freedom to be.

It is in those moments that I touch eternity, know transcendence, and meet God. That is the place where I believe I enter a reality that is not bound by finitude. Eternity lives in me just as God lives in me. I am a part of who God is, or as Meister Eckhart observed in the 14th century, "my me is God." No, that is not a statement of arrogant, modern megalomania. It is rather the discovery of the doorway into a Christianity that will emerge in the coming reformation in which a new God-consciousness, beyond the theistic limits of yesterday, will be born. I await the Reformation! I hope I have contributed to its arrival!

Periodical Bibliography

The following articles have been selected to supplement the diverse views presented in this chapter.

Alan Abel — "Soul Survivors," *Saturday Night*, September 1998.

John Elvin — "In Search of the Soul," *Insight on the News*, September 10, 2001.

Bruce Goldberg — "Hypnotic Highways," *Fate*, August 1997.

Bruce J. Horacek — "Amazing Grace: The Healing Effects of Near-Death Experiences on Those Dying and Grieving," *Journal of Near-Death Studies*, Winter 1997.

Leslie Alan Horvitz — "More Americans Than Ever Embrace the Hereafter Now," *Insight on the News*, September 22, 1997.

Brendan I. Koerner — "Is There Life After Death?" *U.S. News & World Report*, March 31, 1997.

Laura Darlene Lansberry — "First-Person Report: A Skeptic's Near-Death Experience," *Skeptical Inquirer*, Summer 1994.

Mitchell B. Liester — "Inner Communications Following the Near-Death Experience," *Journal of Near-Death Studies*, Summer 1998.

Bruce Moen — "A Voyage to Knowledge of the Afterlife," *NEXUS*, April/May 1999.

Jonathan Rosen — "Rewriting the End: Elizabeth Kubler-Ross," *New York Times Magazine*, January 22, 1995.

Steven J. Rosen — "Religious Roots of Reincarnation," *Fate*, May 1998.

Shankar Vedantam — "Near Proof for Near-Death?" *Washington Post*, December 17, 2001.

Richard Wiseman et al. — "The Psychology of the Seance, From Experiment to Drama," *Skeptical Inquirer*, March/April 1999.

For Further Discussion

Chapter 1

1. Melissa Pollak contends that belief in UFOs, ghosts, ESP, and other paranormal phenomena is unscientific, and that the popularity of the supernatural reveals a decline in critical thinking skills among Americans. Peter A. Sturrock argues that any phenomenon can be examined with scientific techniques and that serious researchers should avoid labeling so-called supernatural events as beyond the pale of scientific inquiry. Which author do you agree with? Why?

2. Paul Kurtz maintains that reports about allegedly paranormal events should be approached with skepticism, particularly since there is no scientific evidence that supports the existence of such phenomena. In Henry H. Bauer's view, what stance should investigators take regarding paranormal phenomena? How do you think Bauer would respond to Kurtz's argument? Defend your answer using examples from the text.

Chapter 2

1. Joe Nickell argues that so-called hauntings are actually the result of fantasies, waking dreams, hoaxes, or simple perceptual errors. J. Michael Krivyanski, however, writes that ghost investigators have used scientific instruments to record evidence about hauntings. Do you believe that such data is convincing proof of the existence of ghosts? Why or why not? Support your answer with examples from the readings in this anthology.

2. Dean Radin maintains that he has scientific proof that an unconscious "sixth sense" exists, while Michael Shermer contends that no data has yet verified the existence of human psychic ability. What evidence does each author provide to support his argument? Which author's evidence is more convincing? Why?

3. After reading the viewpoints by Jim Marrs and Robert L. Park, are you more likely or less likely to believe allegations that the U.S. government is covering up evidence about the existence of extraterrestrials? Explain.

Chapter 3

1. Clifford A. Pickover suggests that there is intelligent life on other planets because the same physical and chemical forces that brought about life on Earth exist throughout the universe. Mark Wolverton maintains that the evolution of life depends on such a complex convergence of factors that the existence of intelli-

gent beings elsewhere is unlikely. Do you agree or disagree with Wolverton that the complexity of factors enabling evolution casts doubt on the existence of intelligent aliens? Support your answer with evidence from the text.

2. Philip J. Klass argues that the vast majority of UFOs can be explained as natural occurrences and therefore scientists should remain skeptical about the existence of alien spacecraft. In Greg Sandow's discussion of his experiences as a UFO investigator, what possible mundane explanations does he consider? In his view, why should scientists maintain open minds about the possibility of extraterrestrial spacecraft?

3. John E. Mack maintains that the phenomenon of alien abduction is real, while Samuel McCracken contends that the abduction phenomenon is the result of hoaxes or delusions. Mack is a psychiatry professor at Harvard Medical School, and McCracken is an assistant to the chancellor at Boston University. Does knowing the backgrounds of these authors influence your assessment of their arguments? Why or why not?

Chapter 4

1. James J. Booker III contends that near-death experiences are proof that life after death exists. Does the viewpoint by the editors of the *Harvard Health Letter* effectively refute Booker's argument? Why or why not?

2. Prior to reading the viewpoint by John S. Spong, what did you assume would be the contemporary Christian stance on the existence of an afterlife? Did reading this article change your understanding of the Christian viewpoint? Explain your response.

Organizations to Contact

The editors have compiled the following list of organizations concerned with the issues debated in this book. The descriptions are derived from materials provided by the organizations. All have publications or information available for interested readers. The list was compiled on the date of publication of the present volume; the information provided here may change. Be aware that many organizations take several weeks or longer to respond to inquiries, so allow as much time as possible.

Academy of Religion and Psychical Research (ARPR)
PO Box 614, Bloomfield, CT 06002-0614
(860) 242-4593
e-mail: batyb@infi.net • website: www.lightlink.com/arpr

Formed in 1972, the ARPR encourages the exchange of ideas among clergy, scientists, and academics in the fields of religion, philosophy, history, and the humanities. Focusing specifically on where the fields of religion and psychical research interface, the academy views parapsychology as providing an authoritative model of empirical science as well as having a bearing upon religious claims. It publishes the scholarly quarterly *Journal of Psychical Research* and the quarterly newsletter *ARPR Bulletin*.

American Association for Parapsychology (AAP)
PO Box 225, Canoga Park, CA 91305
(818) 883-0840 • fax: (818) 884-1850
website: www.parapsychologydegrees.com

The AAP strives to provide a better understanding of the scientific basis for psychic phenomena and to utilize this knowledge for the betterment of humankind. Through its comprehensive study course on the science of parapsychology, the association attempts to bridge the gap between psychic research in the natural and social sciences with that of research in philosophy and comparative religion. It publishes various outlines and research guides, including "A Guide for Understanding Parapsychology."

American Society for Psychical Research (ASPR)
5 W. 73rd St., New York, NY 10023
(212) 799-5050 • fax: (212) 496-2497
e-mail: aspr@aspr.com • website: www.aspr.com

The ASPR was founded in 1895 by a group of scholars who endeavored to explore the uncharted realms of human consciousness, including unexplained phenomena that have been called psychic or paranormal. Through its research and educational programs, the society supports the efforts of both laypersons and professionals to use the study of psychic phenomena to expand and improve the understanding of human nature and the broad scope of human abilities. The ASPR publishes the quarterly *Journal of the American Society for Psychical Research* as well as numerous books and audio and videotapes.

Borderland Sciences Research Foundation (BSRF)
PO Box 6250, Eureka, CA 95502
(707) 445-2247 • fax: (707) 445-1401
e-mail: mail@borderland.com • website: www.borderland.com

The BSRF is composed of individuals interested in investigating realms normally beyond the range of basic human perception and physical measurement. It attempts to explore phenomena that orthodox science either cannot or will not investigate. Among the foundation's numerous publications are the quarterly *Journal of Borderland Research* and the books *Extraterrestrial Archeology: Incredible Proof We Are Not Alone* and *The Cosmic Pulse of Life: The Revolutionary Biological Power Behind UFOs*.

Center for the Study of Extraterrestrial Intelligence (CSETI)
PO Box 265, Crozet, VA 22932-0265
(301) 249-3915
website: www.cseti.org

CSETI is a nonprofit research and educational organization that is dedicated to establishing peaceful and sustainable contact with extraterrestrial lifeforms. It also works to educate society about extraterrestrial intelligence. The center publishes numerous position papers, such as "Understanding UFO Secrecy" and "Abductions: Not All That Glitters Is Gold," as well as field reports on UFOs.

Citizens Against UFO Secrecy, Inc. (CAUS)
PO Box 20351, Sedona, AZ 86341-0351
(602) 818-8248
website: www.caus.org

CAUS is a nonprofit public interest group that believes that extraterrestrial intelligence is in contact with Earth and that there is a campaign of secrecy to conceal this knowledge. Its goals are to educate and enlighten the public about this cover-up and to fund further research into extraterrestrial contact with Earth. It publishes the quarterly newsletter *Just Cause* and the book *Clear Intent*.

Committee for the Scientific Investigation of Claims of the Paranormal (CSICOP)
PO Box 703, Amherst, NY 14226
(716) 636-1425 • fax: (716) 636-1733
e-mail: info@csicop.org • website: www.csicop.org
Established in 1976, the committee is a nonprofit scientific and educational organization that encourages the critical investigation of paranormal and fringe-science claims from a scientific point of view. It disseminates factual information about the results of such inquiries to the scientific community and the public. CSICOP publishes *Skeptical Inquirer* magazine, the children's book *Bringing UFOs Down to Earth*, and bibliographies of other published materials that examine claims of the paranormal.

Federal Bureau of Investigation (FBI)
Headquarters
J. Edgar Hoover Building
935 Pennsylvania Ave. NW, Washington, DC 20535-0001
(202) 324-3000
website: www.fbi.gov
The FBI hosts an official website that includes, among other things, an electronic reading room. The reading room offers all published FBI findings and articles on UFOs, with such topics as "Animal/Cattle Mutilation," and "Roswell."

International Association for Near-Death Studies (IANDS)
PO Box 502, East Windsor Hill, CT 06028
(860) 528-5144 • fax: (860) 528-9169
website: www.iands.org/iands
IANDS is a worldwide organization of scientists, scholars, and others who are interested in or who have had near-death experiences. It supports the scientific study of near-death experiences and their implications, fosters communication among researchers on this topic, and sponsors support groups in which people can discuss their near-death experiences. The association publishes the quarterly newsletter *Vital Signs*.

J. Allen Hynek Center for UFO Studies (CUFOS)
2457 W. Peterson Ave., Chicago, IL 60659
(773) 271-3611
e-mail: infocenter@cufos.org • website: www.cufos.org
CUFOS is a nonprofit scientific organization dedicated to the continuing examination and analysis of the UFO phenomenon. The center acts as a clearinghouse for the reporting and researching of

UFO experiences. It publishes the quarterly *International UFO Reporter*, the *Journal of UFO Studies*, monographs, and special reports.

Mutual UFO Network (MUFON)
130 Oldtowne Rd., Seguin, TX 78155-4099
(210) 379-9216 • fax: (210) 372-9439
e-mail: mufonq@aol.com • website: www.mufon.org
Canadian website: www.renaissoft.com/ufocanada/

MUFON is the world's largest civilian UFO research organization. MUFON documents, investigates, and studies cases of UFO sightings and alien encounters. It also holds conferences and symposiums on UFO-related issues. Its members include well-known ufologists and abductees, as well as physicians, psychiatrists, psychologists, astronomers, theologians, engineers, and other scientific professionals. It publishes the *MUFON UFO Journal* and *Symposium Proceedings*, which contain reports on its conferences.

National UFO Reporting Center
PO Box 45623, University Station, Seattle, WA 98145
UFO Report Hot Line: (206) 722-3000
website: www.ufocenter.com

Founded in 1974, the center serves as a headquarters for reporting possible UFO sightings. Such reports are recorded and disseminated for objective research and information purposes. The center maintains an online database of all reports and also publishes a monthly newsletter.

Parapsychology Foundation, Inc.
228 East 71st Street, New York, NY 10021
(212) 628-1550 • fax: (212) 628-1559
website: www.parapsychology.org

The Parapsychology Foundation is a nonprofit organization that promotes and supports impartial scientific inquiry into the psychic aspects of human nature. It encourages scientific investigators to pursue independent studies of the human mind and it acts as a clearinghouse for parapsychological information. The foundation maintains the Eileen J. Garret Library, which houses a collection of more than 10,000 volumes and 100 periodicals on parapsychology and related topics. It also publishes pamphlets, monographs, conference proceedings, and the *International Journal of Parapsychology*.

Rhine Research Center and Institute for Parapsychology
402 N. Buchanan Blvd., Durham, NC 27701-1728
(919) 688-8241 • fax: (919) 683-4338
e-mail: info@rhine.org • website: www.rhine.org

As successor to the Duke University Parapsychology Laboratory, the Rhine Research Center is a research and educational organization established to explore unusual types of experiences that suggest capabilities yet unrecognized in the human mind. It seeks to bridge gaps between the academic community and independent researchers and between the general public and the research laboratory. Among the center's numerous publications are the quarterly *Journal of Parapsychology* and the books *Explaining the Unexplained: Mysteries of the Paranormal*, and *What Survives? Contemporary Explorations of Life After Death*.

SETI Institute
2035 Landings Dr., Mountain View, CA 94043
(650) 961-6633 • fax: (650) 961-7099
website: www.seti-inst.edu

The SETI Institute is a scientific organization that conducts the world's most comprehensive search for extraterrestrial intelligence. The radio telescopes used in its Project Phoenix scan nearby stars, searching for radio signals from other planets. Its goal is to map the origin, prevalence, and distribution of life in the universe. The institute publishes the newsletter *SETI News*.

Skeptics Society
PO Box 338, Altadena, CA 91001
(818) 794-3119 • fax: (818) 794-1301
e-mail: skepticmag@aol.com • website: www.skeptic.com

The society is composed of scholars, scientists, and historians who promote the use of scientific methods to scrutinize such nonscientific beliefs as religion, superstition, mysticism, and New Age tenets. It is devoted to the investigation of extraordinary claims and revolutionary ideas and to the promotion of science and critical thinking. The society publishes the quarterly *Skeptic Magazine*.

Society for Scientific Exploration
PO Box 3818, Charlottesville, VA 22903
fax: (804) 924-4905
e-mail: sims@jse.com • website: www.jse.com

Affiliated with the University of Virginia's Department of Astronomy, the society seeks to provide a professional forum for presentations, criticisms, and debates concerting topics that are ignored or given inadequate study by mainstream academia. It strives to increase understanding of the factors that at present limit the scope of scientific inquiry. The society publishes the quarterly *Journal of Scientific Exploration* and *Explorer*.

Bibliography of Books

Henry H. Bauer — *Science or Pseudoscience: Magnetic Healing, Psychic Phenomena, and Other Heterodoxies.* Urbana: University of Illinois Press, 2001.

Phillip L. Berman — *The Journey Home: What Near-Death Experiences and Mysticism Teach Us About the Gift of Life.* New York: Pocket, 1998.

David J. Darling — *Zen Physics: The Science of Death, the Logic of Reincarnation.* New York: HarperCollins, 1996.

Jodi Dean — *Aliens in America: Conspiracy Cultures from Outerspace to Cyberspace.* Ithaca, NY: Cornell University Press, 1998.

Keith DeRose and Ted A. Warfield, eds. — *Skepticism: A Contemporary Reader.* New York: Oxford University Press, 1999.

Paul Devereux and Peter Brookesmith — *UFOs and Ufology: The First 50 Years.* New York: Facts On File, 1997.

Paul Edwards — *Reincarnation: A Critical Examination.* Buffalo, NY: Prometheus, 1996.

Randall Fitzgerald — *Cosmic Test Tube: Extraterrestrial Contact, Theories and Evidence.* Los Angeles: Moon Lake Media, 1998.

Fred M. Frohock — *Lives of the Psychics: The Shared Worlds of Science and Mysticism.* Chicago: University of Chicago Press, 2000.

H. Leon Green — *If I Should Wake Before I Die: The Medical and Biblical Truth About Near-Death Experiences.* Wheaton, IL: Crossway, 1997.

Brian Innes — *Death and the Afterlife.* New York: St. Martin's, 1999.

David M. Jacobs — *The Threat.* New York: Simon and Schuster, 1998.

David M. Jacobs, ed. — *UFOs and Abductions: Challenging the Borders of Knowledge.* Lawrence: University Press of Kansas, 2000.

Wendy Kaminer — *Sleeping with Extra-Terrestrials: The Rise of Irrationalism and Perils of Piety.* New York: Pantheon Books, 1999.

Philip J. Klass — *The Real Roswell Crashed-Saucer Coverup.* Amherst, NY: Prometheus, 1997.

John E. Mack — *Passport to the Cosmos.* New York: Crown, 1999.

Joe Nickell, Barry Karr, and Tome Genoni, eds.	*The Outer Edge: Classic Investigations of the Paranormal.* Amherst, NY: Committee for the Scientific Investigation of Claims of the Para- normal, 1996.
Phil Patton	*Dreamland: Travels Inside the Secret World of Roswell and Area 51.* New York: Villard, 1998.
Kevin D. Randle, Russ Estes, and William P. Cone	*The Abduction Enigma.* New York: Tom Doherty Associates, Inc., 1999.
Ron Roberts and David Grooms	*Parapsychology: The Science of Unusual Experience.* London: Arnold, 2000.
Barbara Rommer	*Blessing in Disguise: Another Side of the Near-Death Experience.* St. Paul, MN: Llewellyn, 2000.
Michael Shermer	*Why People Believe Weird Things: Pseudoscience, Superstition, and Other Confusions of Our Time.* New York: W.H. Freeman and Company, 1997.
Starhawk and Macha NightMare, eds.	*The Pagan Book of Living and Dying: Practical Rituals, Blessings, and Meditations on Crossing Over.* New York: HarperCollins, 1998.
Nancy H. Traill	*Possible Worlds of the Fantastic: The Rise of the Paranormal in Fiction.* Toronto: University of Toronto Press, 1996.
Evelyn Elsaesser Valarino	*On the Other Side of Life: Exploring the Phenomenon of the Near-Death Experience.* New York: Plenum Books, 1997.
Richard L. Weaver and James McAndrew	*The Roswell Report: Case Closed.* Written on behalf of Headquarters United States Air Force. Washington, DC: Government Printing Office, 1995.
William F. Williams, ed.	*Encyclopedia of Pseudoscience.* New York: Facts on File, 2000.

Index